"Kim is my go-to cold call when I need guidance on a menu. She is my culinary Google Maps and the most fun person to dine with. Long live Kim!"

—**TRIXIE MATTEL,** skinny legend and drag mogul

"Kim Chi's approach to cooking is similar to her approach to drag: bold, colorful, encouraging, and globally inspired. This book is a great introduction to some of the best cuisines in the world for anyone looking to expand their pantry and shake up mealtime. All the recipes tell the story of Kim Chi's life while encouraging the reader to play in their own kitchens. It belongs on the shelves of curious cooks everywhere."

—**KHUSHBU SHAH,** contributing editor for *Food & Wine* and author of *Amrikan*

"Kim Chi is the only person I know who loves food more than me, and *Kim Chi Eats the World* truly showcases that passion! Not only are the recipes delicious, fun, and diverse, the stories are also wonderfully entertaining, thoughtful, and funny. This cookbook is everything you want and expect from everyone's favorite drag queen!"

—**RONNIE WOO,** celebrity chef and bestselling author of *Did You Eat Yet?*

KIM CHI
EATS
THE WORLD

KIM CHI EATS THE WORLD

75 Recipes Fit for a (Drag) Queen

KIM CHI

Photographs by Andrea D'Agosto

UNION SQUARE & CO.
NEW YORK

UNION SQUARE & CO.
NEW YORK

UNION SQUARE & CO. and the distinctive Union Square & Co. logo are trademarks of Hachette Book Group, Inc.

ISBN 978-1-4549-5626-6
ISBN 978-1-4549-5627-3 (e-book)

Union Square & Co. books may be purchased in bulk for business, educational, or promotional use. For more information, please contact your local bookseller or the Hachette Book Group's Special Markets department at special.markets@hbgusa.com.

Printed in Malaysia

10 9 8 7 6 5 4 3 2 1

unionsquareandco.com

Editor: Amanda Englander
Assistant Editor: Juliana Nador
Designer: Renée Bollier
Photographer: Andrea D'Agosto
Food Stylist: Tyna Hoang
Prop Stylist: Ruth Kim
Project Editor: Ivy McFadden
Production Manager: Terence Campo
Copy Editor: Mark McCauslin

Additional image credits:
Page 10: Santiago Felipe/Getty Images Entertainment
Shutterstock.com: Viktoriia Ablohina: 24–25, 62–63, 88–89, 142–143 (BW frames); Olive Kitt: throughout (stickers): Olniz: cover, 7, 9, 15, 19, 21, 22, 60, 86, 140 (color frames); Xenia Artwork: throughout (stickers)

To my fans:
Thanks for believing in me and booking me, so I can eat my way around the world.

CONTENTS

I've always been in love with food.

Food has never ghosted me, cheated on me, or shown up late (unless we're talking about delivery apps, but that's another story). From my childhood, which stretched across two continents, to my career jet-setting as a drag queen, I've learned that food is more than just calories and carbs—it's culture, history, and, most important, a delicious excuse to avoid small talk.

When you start to dig into the way a dish is prepared in any corner of the world, you're not just tasting food—you're tasting the story of their traditions, climate, religion, trade, colonization (the audacity!), and survival. Basically, every bite is an edible Wikipedia entry, minus the boring footnotes. And if there's one thing I've learned from dragging my suitcase through unforgettable small towns, crowded night markets, and hole-in-the wall spots, it's that the best meals are found where you least expect them—just like a fierce drag performance at your local bar on a Monday night. (Support local drag!)

I was born in Lansing, Michigan: the heart of the Rust Belt of the United States, which is as unglamorous as it sounds. When I was five years old, my dad finished his PhD and moved our family back to Korea to work as a professor. That's where I first learned that food isn't just something you eat—it's an event and an experience. All of my earliest memories started there, where I was surrounded by the spices, sauces, meats, vegetables, and seafood central to Korean cooking. Dishes like Birthday Seaweed Soup (page 147) and Bossam (page 153) still send me right back to my childhood. Korean cooking is like drag: bold, unapologetic, and always leaving you wanting more.

When we moved back to the United States when I was twelve, well, let's just say it was . . . a *vibe*. Michigan didn't exactly roll out the red carpet for my taste buds. Suddenly, I was in a

land where people thought "seasoning" meant adding more ranch dressing. Not only did I have to learn a language I had left behind, but I also had to learn how to relate to American culture and eat with an American palate.

But, being the enterprising queen I am, I wasn't about to let bland food get the best of me. I saved my allowance, skipped lunch at school (trust me, I wasn't missing much), and started exploring restaurants around town with my "dining budget." I convinced my friends to try Thai and Ethiopian restaurants, places that were exploding with new flavors. I was lucky to have a diverse group of friends whose families invited me over for dinner, introducing me to Indian and Mexican home cooking that was better than any restaurant—and better than the Midwestern staples that were a true culture shock to my system . . . and my stomach. My mom worked nights at a Korean restaurant while she raised my little brother and me. Which meant I had to take on the role of family chef—which *actually* meant I experimented on my brother with whatever recipes I could half remember from culinary field trips. (He had to do the dishes, so he resented some of my saucier experiments.) Yogurt Rice (page 206) and Dal Tadka (page 209) were a few of my earliest specialties. I was learning and my brother didn't die, so I'll call it a win.

At age nineteen, I left home and moved to Chicago for art school. After school ended, I began working as a graphic designer while also supporting myself as a server in a fine-dining restaurant, aka the city rent hustle. When you're working in fine-dining, part of the job is tasting all the food the kitchen serves so you can accurately represent every component of every dish to every diner. The work was tough, but that exposure to chef-driven cooking—and ingredients I had definitely never tried back in Michigan—was my first real training in all things culinary, and it began to expand the way I see food and educate my palate. (My recipe for Pulled Pork Cornbread Benedict, page 35, is a love letter to my time there.)

Just like waiting tables was never part of the plan, my journey into drag wasn't exactly on the menu either. But what is life without a plot twist? Like many queens before and after me, drag first came into my life on Halloween. A friend and I decided to go all out, bought clown makeup at CVS (classic), and accidentally stumbled into a drag show. The booker loved our looks and asked us to come back to perform the following week. Of course we said yes! I didn't have a performance background, so I was terrified. I lip-synced to "Stop" by the Spice Girls, and I should have taken the message of the song more seriously. If I were to describe that first performance with two words they would be: A Mess. But I guess I looked cute enough, because soon I was hosting parties around town, which basically meant dressing up in a fierce look, bullying your friends into coming to the event, and walking around high on the power of drink tickets. You know how it is—one minute you're a server, the next you're the queen of Boystown.

About a year and a half into my new drag career, on a whim, I applied for season eight of *RuPaul's Drag Race*. I had been a huge fan of the show from the start, and two close friends of mine had already been on it. (I won't name names, but they rhyme with Pixie Unwell and Hurl.) So I thought, why not? The audition process was more straightforward during my season, so I put together my audition tape in a week and sent it in. I was shocked when I got selected. Anyone who has been on the show (or probably any competition reality show) will tell you the stress of filming makes the entire experience a total blur. *Drag Race* was a small show on a premium cable channel, and drag was still growing in public consciousness, but from the moment the cast was announced, I was no longer just a drag queen. I was a Ru Girl. And I was about to travel all over the world.

During filming, donuts accidentally became my brand. In the first episode, there's a clip of me joking around with one of the producers in the confessional room. Apropos of nothing, I said, "Donut come for me . . ." just to make everyone laugh. The clip made it to air, and suddenly everywhere I went, at every gig and every hotel, boxes and boxes of donuts were waiting for me. (I hope you're not disappointed that there's no donut recipe in this book. I need a break. Thank you for respecting my privacy at this time!) This was the first time drag and food intersected for me, but it was only the start.

After season eight ended, my life became a blur of no sleep: bus, club, another club, another club, plane, onto the next place; repeat. I was zigzagging across North and South America, all over Asia, and touching down in Europe on the way to the next stop. Because of the hectic schedule—sometimes arriving, performing, and leaving all within twenty-four hours—I was eating every meal out. I started to plan my travel so I'd have at least one afternoon or evening to myself in each location. Even when the accumulated jet lag and late nights wanted to win, I fought to find the energy to get out and explore each city. I've always wanted to tour the world on someone else's dime, so I wasn't going to waste a second.

The chance to try the street food, restaurants, and specialties of each place made me feel more connected to where I was in those moments, however fleeting they were. Food is one of the strongest ways to build memories, and those memories became my treasured souvenirs. Eating my way around the world became the best part of my career. I was obsessed with finding new textures, flavors, and styles I hadn't yet experienced. Dishes like Custardy Soft Scrambled Eggs (page 102) in Paris or Laksa Noodle Soup (page 180) in Singapore forever changed my palate. And between shows, on all those endless flights, I was basically a research machine. Believe it or not, Twitter was my secret weapon—ask the fans for recs and they'll always pull through.

When the pandemic hit in 2020, my travel came to a sudden stop. No more planes, no more hotel rooms, no more greasy late-night bites. (Trust me, queens know their way around a twenty-four-hour diner menu like nobody else.) Instead, I was stuck at home, like so many others, rediscovering the kitchen. It was the first time in years that I actually had time to cook, and, as dramatic as it sounds, it was life-changing. I started re-creating all the incredible meals I'd had around the world, and my monthly trip to the grocery store was the best form of retail therapy. Cooking took me back to those moments, like a chippy-shop-style order of Curry and Chips (page 91) after the club in London. Searing skewers of Moo Ping (page 188) made me feel like I was at a bustling, smoky Thai street stall. I started writing down my ideas, inspirations, and recipes so I would be able to take myself everywhere without going anywhere whenever I felt like it. I didn't know it then, but those notes were the beginning of this book.

It's funny how drag and food overlap. Both are about creativity, storytelling, and, most of all, a little drama. When it comes to blending eyeshadow or blending spices, I want everything to be just right. But what really ties drag and food together is the way they both unite people. Let me tell you, nothing will get your friends over faster than the promise of a Cheesy Bread Bowl Fondue (page 134) or a steaming pot of Budae Jjigae (page 149). When I'm in the kitchen, I like my cooking the way I like my drag: bold, colorful, and always with a touch of humor, because whether I'm serving up a lqqk or a whole meal, I always want it to be full of flavor, personality, and heart.

This book is a collection of recipes and stories that mean the world (literally) to me. From the Korean dishes that remind me of my childhood to the global flavors I've picked up during my travels, these recipes represent my journey, my heritage, and my love for food. While, of course, every country on basically every continent has its own delectable and distinctive food culture, these are simply all of the countries I visited while on tour and some of my favorite meals I had on those visits. Some are simple comfort foods that you'll love to make on a lazy Sunday. Others are a bit more extravagant, perfect for a dinner party that calls for extra drama (and maybe a wig or two!). Just like drag, cooking is all about experimenting, making mistakes, and laughing at yourself along the way. Whether you're an experienced home cook or just getting started, I hope these recipes inspire you to get in the kitchen, try something new, and, most important, have fun. Because if there's one thing I've learned from drag and from cooking, it's this: The messiest moments usually end up being the most memorable.

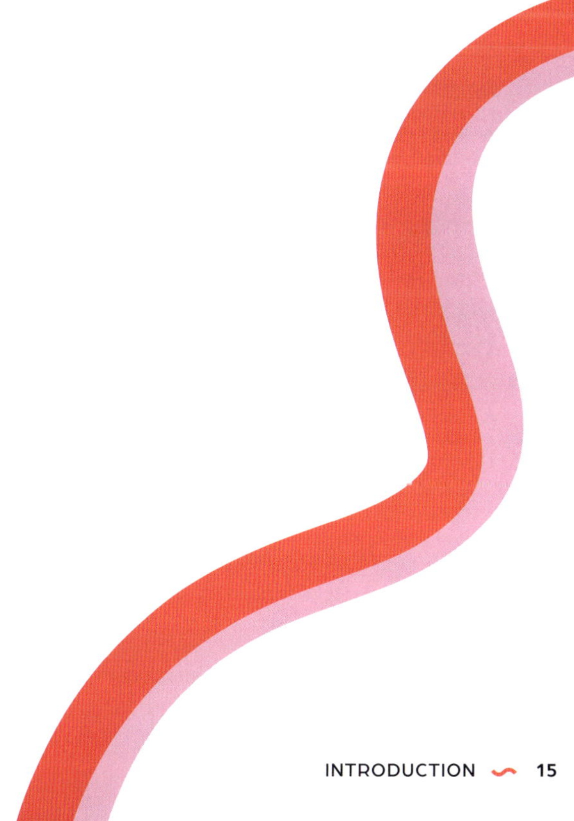

NUOC MAM NHI
Việt Hươn
FISH SAUCE
Hamdard
Rooh Afza
28.22 FL OZ
CENTO
NONGSHIM
辛
라면
SHIN
NOODLES
SESAME
2-WAY
CHEF CAP
KEWPIE
MAYONNAISE
EZ SQUEEZE TUBE
12 FL OZ
(355mL)
CALPICO
mini
original
SAVOY
COCONUT CREAM
AUTHENTIC KOREAN
KIMCHI
NAPA CABBAGE
SPICY
Nestlé
Carnation
the cooking milk
BETTER THAN BOUIL
MADE WITH SEASONED ROASTED
순창
MAE PLOY
SWEET CHILLI SAUCE
content 10 fl oz (280 mL)
PRODUCT OF ITALY
ORGANIC TOMATO PASTE
AYAM
SPICE PASTE
FOR LAKSA
CURRY NOODLE
DYNASTY
Sliced
Bamboo Shoots
food
순창
해찬들
GOCHUJANG
HOT PEPPER PASTE
매운맛 고추장
NET WT. 17.63 oz (1.10 lb) 500g
No.1
WONDER
CALCIUM FORTIFIED ENRICHED BREAD
NET WT 20 OZ (1 LB 4 OZ) 567g
BEAVER
Cream
HORSERADISH
Firm
TOF
PERFECT FOR STIR FRY
NET WT. 16OZ.

Crouching Queen, Hidden Condiments

My fridge and pantry are a revolving door of whatever I'm craving at any given moment, but there are a few staples that always make the cut. I think of them as my go-tos, my secret flavor weapons that can pull double or triple duty, no matter what I'm cooking. No need to wade through a sea of ingredients—I've got my top ten all-stars ready to glam up your kitchen and keep your cooking exciting:

SALT: All the recipes in this book were developed with Diamond Crystal kosher salt. (If you're using Morton coarse kosher salt, fine sea salt, or table salt, use half of the listed amount.) Salt is the lifeline of all cooking, the ultimate flavor enhancer for everything sweet and savory. When something's off, a pinch of salt is almost always the right answer (unless, of course, it tastes too salty). And when something needs a crunchy, salty finishing touch, I use a flaky sea salt, like Maldon.

WHITE PEPPER: When I want something smoother than the sharp, overwhelming flavor of freshly cracked black pepper, I reach for my jar of white pepper instead. Sold as a ground spice, white pepper has a softer and more floral flavor than black pepper, and less bite. It can slip into any dish without much fanfare and help season the dish more evenly.

GARLIC: This is the world's great unifier. No matter what cuisine you're cooking, garlic is probably involved in some capacity. I have multiple types in stock at all times: full bulbs, pre-peeled cloves, minced in a jar, pureed in a tube, even frozen and cubed. I use them all in rotation. Get whatever is most useful to you and the recipe you're following.

AVOCADO OIL: This is extra-virgin olive oil's harder-working cousin. It has a gentler, more neutral flavor than olive oil, plus a much higher smoke point—which means it's perfect for high-heat pan-frying, roasting, grilling, and even baking. But it can also be used just like olive oil in dressings and dipping sauces. Throughout the book, I'll say "olive oil," but just know I'm secretly using avocado oil—feel free to use an alternative like safflower or grapeseed oil.

GRANULATED SUGAR: Cooking is all about balance, so even savory things benefit from a little sweetness. I like granulated sugar because it has a subtle flavor and dissolves quickly, making it easy to mix into dry rubs, sauces, and creamy dressings.

SOY SAUCE: Put it to work marinating meats, enhancing Thanksgiving gravy, upping the umami in marinara sauce, seasoning burgers, roasting nuts—anything that needs a savory saltiness can use a splash of soy sauce! If regular soy sauce is too salty for you, just thin it out with a little water or rice vinegar.

FISH SAUCE: Another savory powerhouse, I add a splash of fish sauce to enhance soup broths, add balance to vinaigrettes and dressings, replace anchovies in a pasta sauce, and give steamed vegetables an umami punch.

UNSEASONED RICE VINEGAR: I may be biased, but this is the best all-purpose vinegar. It has a sweet, subtle flavor, which means it can add acidity without taking over. It's always in my vinaigrettes, marinades, homemade pickles, and sauces, but it's also perfect for a little acidity in cocktails or splashed over hot, crispy french fries.

GOCHUJANG: This Korean fermented chile paste is a miracle of savory, sweet, and spicy flavors. I like to mix it into barbecue sauces, toss with hot chicken wings, rub on vegetables before roasting, or whisk with mayo for a spicy dipping sauce.

GOCHUGARU: Korea's signature red pepper flakes are fruity, smoky, and sweet, giving everything a much more complex flavor than the red pepper flakes hanging out in most pantries. I use these in the exact same way: to build flavor in soups, stews, and stir-fries; whisked in scrambled eggs; and even sprinkled on popcorn and pizza. A little goes a long way.

BONUS: KIMCHI! This goes without saying, but I'll say it anyway: Kimchi is the center of my universe. I put it on everything—tacos, fried rice, hot dogs, eggs, soups, grilled meats. But most of all, I love to serve it as a small side dish (known as *banchan* in Korean) to enjoy alongside any meal.

KIM CHI'S

QUICK KIMCHI

When most people hear the word *kimchi*, they think of one of two things: me or cabbage. But did you know you can kimchi almost anything? When I'm in a rush (or just too hangry to wait), I make this quick and easy tomato kimchi. It's tangy and refreshing, packing all the flavor of traditional kimchi without the wait. Plus, the burst of juicy tomatoes makes it the perfect side dish for just about any meal. Try it once and you'll be saying, "Cabbage who?"

Makes 1 quart

- ¼ cup gochugaru
- ¼ cup fish sauce
- 1 tablespoon sugar
- 1 tablespoon maesilaek (see Note)
- 8 garlic cloves, minced
- 6 beefsteak tomatoes, cut into wedges, or 3 cups cherry tomatoes, halved
- 1 large white onion, diced
- Handful of chives, cut into 1-inch pieces
- Sesame seeds, for garnish

In a large bowl, whisk the gochugaru, fish sauce, sugar, maesilaek, and garlic to combine. Add the tomatoes, onions, and chives and toss to coat in the sauce. Sprinkle a generous amount of sesame seeds on top. Cover the bowl tightly with plastic wrap and refrigerate for at least 2 hours and up to 1 week before serving.

NOTE: Maesilaek, a sweet and sour syrup made from fermented green plums, can be found in Korean grocery stores or online. It can also be substituted with apple juice or pear juice.

Break the Rules, Make It Delicious

My favorite part of traveling is the exposure to flavors and ideas that I've never experienced before. My souvenirs are the memories of what I ate, and I try to re-create that feeling in my own kitchen. That's all to say: These are not authentic recipes! They are *my take* on dishes I love, but nothing in this book is a hard and fast rule. I wrote these recipes to share the experiences I've had, and also to encourage you to expand your palate and learn new culinary techniques, all while using ingredients and methods that are within reach of the average home cook.

You know how everyone thinks their mom's version of something is the best version? That's how everyone thinks in every country, which means there are thousands of "correct" ways to make any traditional recipe. The most important thing is that the outcome tastes good to you, and even better if it's something you want to eat again. Add sugar and salt where you feel like you need it. If you're sensitive to spice, leave it out. Don't stress about finding every last ingredient—swap in something you already have or skip it. Take bits and pieces from different dishes to Frankenstein your dream dinner. Recipes are meant to develop and change with time as you make them over and over, adapting and substituting until they become your own.

I did say there are no hard and fast rules in this book, but I forgot there is just one: Cook from your heart! Food should be a joyful experience that you're excited to share with the people you love. That's the best way to take a recipe and turn it into a tradition of your own.

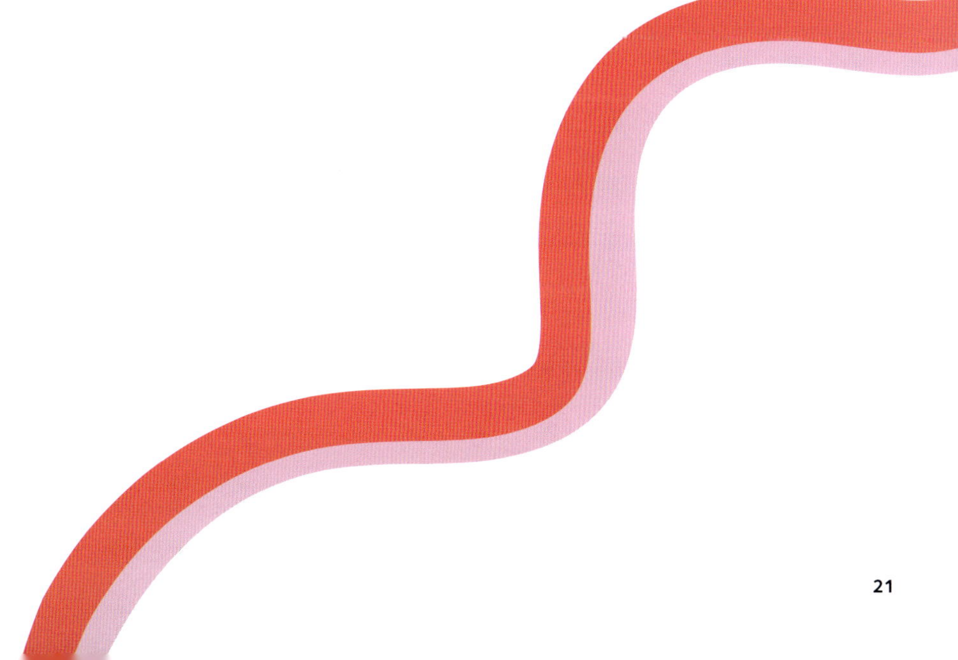

NORTH AMERICA

O Say Can You Eat

My first international gig after *Drag Race* was in Canada, and it's where I still feel the most love from fans. After years of touring, with late-night heaping spoonfuls of poutine and early-morning coffee recoveries at Tim Hortons, a Canadian cultural icon, I could see myself living there one day. (Maybe now more than ever.)

But it was touring the United States that taught me something I hadn't realized previously: This country isn't just endless suburbs filled with Targets and Applebee's (though, honestly, no shade to a good mozzarella stick). Rather, every state has its own culture and every city has its own personality, from San Antonio's cowboy flair to New York's rough charm to Seattle's . . . well, rain. The real star, of course, is the food. There's no topping Creole cuisine in Louisiana or a perfect cheesesteak in Philly or the endless barbecue debates in the South—I don't want to start a fight, so I'll keep my opinions on that to myself.

And then there's Mexico. Taking a taco tour in Mexico City was like stepping into a culinary dream. The fresh ingredients, the meticulous craft—it all blew me away. Puerto Vallarta and Monterrey also brought their A game—there's something magical about eating in a country where every bite tells a story.

North America is a patchwork of personalities—bold, chaotic, and unapologetically extra. Just like a good drag performance, it's full of surprises, and always leaves you wanting more.

Monte Cristo

In high school, my friends and I spent a lot of time at Bennigan's, the Irish pub-themed chain restaurant that was everywhere in the 1990s and early 2000s. I don't remember much about their menu because we were there for one thing and one thing only: the Monte Cristo. Their version was three layers of bread, piled high with ham, turkey, and so much cheese, then fried, coated with powdered sugar, and served with a side of raspberry preserves. So, if you want the most sinful, decadent, and indulgent sandwich ever created (probably followed by a nap after), this recipe is the one to try!

- 1 large egg
- ¼ cup whole milk
- 2 tablespoons unsalted butter
- 3 slices whole-wheat sandwich bread
- 2 tablespoons raspberry jam
- 2 slices cheddar cheese
- 2 slices deli ham
- 2 slices Swiss cheese
- 2 slices deli turkey
- Powdered sugar and maple syrup, for serving

1. In a large shallow bowl, whisk together the egg and milk. In a medium skillet, melt 1 tablespoon of the butter over medium heat. Dip 1 slice of the bread in the egg mixture, turning to coat both sides. Let the excess drip off, then place in the skillet. Cook, flipping once, until both sides are golden brown, about 3 minutes per side. Transfer to a plate.

2. Meanwhile, spread the raspberry jam on one side of the remaining 2 bread slices. In the same skillet, melt the remaining 1 tablespoon butter over medium heat and dip the uncoated sides of the bread into the egg mixture, allowing the excess to drip off. Add both slices to the skillet, egg-side down. On one slice, layer the cheddar cheese and ham on top of the jam. On the other slice, layer the Swiss cheese and turkey on top of the jam. Cover the skillet and cook until the cheeses are melted and the bottom of the bread is golden brown, about 3 minutes.

3. Set the reserved butter-fried slice on top of the ham slice, then flip the turkey slice on top to make a triple-decker sandwich. Cut the sandwich in half diagonally.

4. Transfer to a plate and dust with powdered sugar. Serve with maple syrup drizzled over the top or alongside for dunking.

Rotisserie Chicken Soup

When I was in art school, a big pot of chicken soup was my favorite way to stay warm and cozy during those long Chicago winters. Young and broke, I was always on the hunt for cheap, satisfying stretch meals. Costco's rotisserie chicken was my knight in shining aluminum foil. I would hitch a ride with my friends and use their Costco membership to buy three chickens at a time, freezing the extras for later. I could pull apart the meat to use in a variety of meals and use the bones to make a batch of broth. If you're not about that life, use store-bought broth (which I use here to keep things simple), but if you want to channel broke-me energy, go for homemade. Either way, this is the chicken soup you'll want on repeat all season long.

- 2 tablespoons extra-virgin olive oil
- 3 medium carrots, diced
- 3 celery stalks, diced
- 1 large white onion, diced
- 2 garlic cloves, minced
- Kosher salt and freshly ground black pepper
- 1 tablespoon finely chopped fresh rosemary
- 1 tablespoon fresh thyme leaves
- 1 rotisserie chicken, meat shredded, skin and bones discarded
- 8 cups chicken broth
- 2 cups dried egg noodles (see Note)
- Chopped fresh parsley, for serving

1. In a large Dutch oven, heat the olive oil over medium heat until it shimmers. Add the carrots, celery, onions, garlic, and a big pinch each of salt and pepper. Cook, stirring occasionally, until the vegetables are vibrant in color and soft, about 8 minutes. Stir in the rosemary and thyme until fragrant, about 30 seconds.

2. Add the chicken and broth and bring to a simmer, then add the noodles. Return to a simmer and cook, stirring occasionally, until the noodles are cooked through, about 6 minutes. Taste and adjust the seasoning to your liking.

3. Divide the soup among eight bowls and garnish with parsley before serving. Any leftover soup can be transferred to an airtight container and stored in the refrigerator for up to 5 days or in the freezer for up to 3 months.

NOTE Egg noodles are a classic in chicken soup, but I usually grab whatever dried pasta I have in the pantry. Snap long noodles into smaller pieces or throw in whole shapes!

Secret Weapon Cookies

As a gay who is always working on a summer body that may never come, I'm very protein conscious. And as a drag queen who is always on the go, I need something satisfying I can slip into my purse for hangry emergencies. These cookies are my secret weapon for extra protein and healthy fiber, plus they're filling and delicious as a 1 a.m. dressing-room-meltdown snack. Who knew cookies could be self-care?

- ½ cup sugar
- ¼ cup unsweetened cocoa powder
- ¼ teaspoon kosher salt
- ½ cup whole milk
- 6 tablespoons (¾ stick) unsalted butter
- 2 tablespoons coconut oil
- 1 cup peanut butter, smooth or crunchy
- 1 cup chocolate protein powder
- 3 cups rolled oats

1. Line two baking sheets with parchment paper.
2. In a large saucepan, whisk together the sugar, cocoa powder, and salt. Whisk in the milk, then add the butter and coconut oil. Cook over low heat, whisking continuously, until the sugar dissolves and the mixture begins to simmer. Remove from the heat and whisk in the peanut butter until melted. Use a rubber spatula to fold in the protein powder and oats.
3. Use a ¼-cup measure to scoop 6 cookies onto each prepared baking sheet and use the bottom of the measuring cup to flatten into rounds. Refrigerate until set, about 30 minutes, then stack in a zip-top bag and refrigerate until ready to eat, up to 5 days. The cookies will be firm straight out of the fridge or soft and chewy after sitting at room temperature.

Scallion Cream Cheese Rangoon

MAKES 12 WONTONS

When I was in high school in Michigan, my favorite class was home economics. (I wasn't out yet, but there were definitely signs.) Our teacher did a unit on using a food processor, and one of the first recipes she taught us was a scallion dip. It was simple but so flavorful, and I've been chasing that high ever since. Instead of the typical crab rangoon found at most Chinese restaurants—a fully American invention that's not Chinese at all—I like to make my own version stuffed to the brim with a scallion cream cheese inspired by that dip. You can add lump crabmeat to these if you want, but personally, I don't want anything coming between me and that perfect scallion flavor!

- 1 (8-ounce) package cream cheese, at room temperature
- ½ teaspoon nori flakes (optional)
- ½ teaspoon garlic powder
- 1 teaspoon soy sauce
- 4 scallions, thinly sliced
- Nonstick cooking spray
- 12 wonton wrappers, thawed if frozen
- 4 cups vegetable oil or other neutral oil, for frying
- Simple Duck Sauce (recipe opposite) or store-bought duck sauce, for serving

1. In a medium bowl, stir together the cream cheese, nori flakes (if using), garlic powder, soy sauce, and scallions. Coat a large plate with nonstick spray.

2. Working with one at a time, lay out a wonton wrapper on a clean work surface. Lightly wet one finger and rub it along the edges of the wrapper. Scoop 1 tablespoon of the cream cheese mixture into the center, then pull up the corners of the wonton to the center and pinch the seams shut. Transfer to the coated plate while you repeat with the remaining wrappers and filling. Refrigerate the stuffed wontons for at least 30 minutes or overnight.

3. In a Dutch oven or large saucepan, heat the oil over medium heat until it registers 350°F on an instant-read thermometer, or dip the corner of a wonton into the oil to test. It should start bubbling immediately. Working in batches of four, add the wontons and cook, flipping occasionally, until golden brown all over, about 4 minutes. Transfer to paper towels to drain and repeat with the remaining wontons, allowing the oil to return to temperature between batches.

4. Arrange the wontons on a platter and serve immediately, with the duck sauce alongside for dipping.

Simple Duck Sauce

MAKES ABOUT ½ CUP

⅓ cup apricot preserves

2 teaspoons unseasoned rice vinegar

1 teaspoon soy sauce

In a small bowl, whisk together the preserves, vinegar, and soy sauce. Store in an airtight container in the refrigerator for up to 5 days.

Pulled Pork Cornbread Benedict

Back when I worked as a restaurant server in Chicago, brunch was the bane of my existence—especially since everyone turned into a coffee-drunk monster by 10 a.m. Politeness went out the window and everyone got bossy about their drinks, toast, and eggs, which all had to be prepared to their specifications for it to be a good meal at all. But when this pulled pork cornbread Benedict was on the brunch menu, it was the only time I knew peace. So special and so perfect, it didn't leave any room for anyone to be picky. I love to make it now when friends come over for breakfast or brunch for something comforting, hearty, and just a little bit classy.

PULLED PORK

- 2 pounds pork tenderloin
- ½ teaspoon kosher salt, plus more for the pork
- 2 tablespoons vegetable oil or other neutral oil
- 1½ cups ketchup
- 1 cup packed dark brown sugar
- ½ cup apple cider vinegar
- 2 tablespoons spicy brown mustard
- 2 tablespoons Worcestershire sauce
- 1 teaspoon smoked paprika
- ½ teaspoon garlic powder
- ½ teaspoon onion powder

1. **Make the pulled pork:** Preheat the oven to 350°F.
2. Pat the pork dry with paper towels and season generously with a few good pinches of salt. In a large Dutch oven, heat the vegetable oil over high heat until it shimmers. Add the pork and cook, turning, until browned all over, about 5 minutes total.
3. Meanwhile, in a medium bowl, whisk together the ketchup, brown sugar, vinegar, mustard, Worcestershire sauce, paprika, garlic powder, onion powder, the remaining ½ teaspoon salt, and 1 cup water. When the pork is browned, remove the pot from the heat and pour in the sauce. Turn the pork to coat fully.
4. Cover the pot and transfer it to the oven. Roast for about 2 hours, until the pork is falling apart. Check periodically to flip the pork and add a splash of water as needed if the pan looks too dry.
5. Use two forks to shred the pork and completely coat it in the sauce. Cover the pot to keep the pork hot. (Or let the pork cool completely and store in an airtight container in the refrigerator for up to 4 days. Before serving, reheat the pork in the pot over low heat with a splash of water.)

Recipe and ingredients continue

6 **Make the cornbread:** Preheat the oven to 350°F. Coat a 9 by 13-inch baking dish with nonstick spray.

7 In a large bowl, whisk together the eggs and granulated sugar. Whisk in the milk, butter, baking powder, and salt. Use a rubber spatula to stir in the flour, cornmeal, frozen corn, cheese, and jalapeños until combined. Scrape the batter into the prepared baking dish and smooth out the top.

8 Bake for about 30 minutes, rotating halfway through, until a tester inserted into the center of the cornbread comes out clean. Let cool for 30 minutes before slicing into 12 squares and serving. The cornbread can also be cooled completely, covered tightly with plastic wrap, and stored at room temperature for up to 3 days.

9 To assemble and serve, fill a large skillet with 1½ inches of water. Bring to a boil over high heat. Cover the skillet and turn off the heat. Working with one at a time, crack an egg into a small bowl or ramekin. Remove the lid from the skillet and hold the lip of the bowl at the edge of the skillet before tipping the egg in. Cover while preparing the next egg. Don't crowd the skillet: Up to 6 eggs should comfortably fit; work in batches, if necessary. Let them sit in the water for 4 to 5 minutes, until the whites are firm but the yolks are still runny.

10 Meanwhile, divide the cornbread among as many plates as needed and top each with a good scoop of pulled pork.

11 Carefully remove each egg with a slotted spoon, dabbing the bottom of the spoon on a clean towel to soak up any excess water. Slide an egg on top of each pork pile and garnish with a few cracks of black pepper and a sprinkle of chives. Serve with a bottle of hot sauce, in case anyone wants a spicy kick.

CORNBREAD

- Nonstick cooking spray
- 3 large eggs
- ¼ cup granulated sugar
- 2 cups whole milk
- 1 cup (2 sticks) unsalted butter, melted
- 2 tablespoons baking powder
- 2 teaspoons kosher salt
- 3 cups all-purpose flour
- 1 cup yellow cornmeal
- 1 cup frozen corn
- 8 ounces sharp cheddar cheese, grated
- 4 jalapeños, seeded and minced

- 12 large eggs
- Freshly ground black pepper and thinly sliced fresh chives, for serving
- Hot sauce, for serving (optional)

Homemade Ketchup Potato Chips

Ketchup is one of the best chip flavors, no question. My cousins live in Toronto, and when I was a kid my family would take road trips from Michigan across the border to visit. When we stopped for gas on the Canadian side, we were each allowed to pick one snack. One day I chose a bag of ketchup chips and, after one bite, my life was forever changed. You all know how much I love them, so when I'm in Canada I get a lot of ketchup chips at meet-and-greets. But when my stash runs low, I make my own. They're the perfect way to get my fix without having to go international—and they taste just as good as the real deal.

- 1 (1-pound) russet potato, unpeeled and scrubbed
- ½ cup apple cider vinegar, plus more as needed
- 1 tablespoon light brown sugar
- 2 teaspoons sweet paprika
- 1 teaspoon kosher salt
- ½ teaspoon onion powder
- ½ teaspoon garlic powder
- 2 quarts vegetable oil or other neutral oil

1. Use a mandoline or very sharp knife to slice the potatoes into ⅛-inch-thick planks. Rinse in a colander under cold water until the water runs clear. In a large bowl, combine the potatoes, ½ cup vinegar, and 4 cups water. Soak the potato slices for 30 minutes, then drain and pat dry with paper towels.

2. Meanwhile, in a small bowl, whisk together the brown sugar, paprika, salt, onion powder, and garlic powder.

3. In a Dutch oven or large saucepan, heat the oil over medium heat until it registers 350°F on an instant-read thermometer, or drop a few potatoes in the oil to test. They should start bubbling immediately. Working in 4 small batches, add the potatoes and cook, stirring occasionally, until golden brown all over, 6 to 8 minutes. Use a slotted spoon to transfer them to a wire rack to drain. Repeat with the remaining potatoes, allowing the oil to return to temperature between batches.

4. Transfer all the chips to a serving bowl. Use a spoon to splash a little vinegar around the edge of the bowl and toss the chips to coat so they're a little bit damp but not soggy. Add big pinches of the spice mixture to the bowl while continuously tossing the chips to coat evenly. Serve immediately.

Peameal Bacon Sandwich

Peameal bacon and I met on a food tour in Toronto. I was filming some food content in St. Lawrence Market and, like a cartoon character, my nose led me right to Carousel Bakery, where I encountered the iconic breakfast treat. One bite in, and I realized why Canadians keep this crispy, coated, porky secret to themselves. It's a round of cured pork loin, rolled in cornmeal and pan-fried for a crunchy edge and juicy center. Peameal bacon is hard to find where I live in the States, so using Canadian bacon is close enough. But if you can find the real thing, it's even better! Serve it solo on a roll, or take it to the next level like I do here with eggs and cheese. Either way, this is the breakfast sandwich that'll make you wish you lived closer to the border.

- 3 tablespoons unsalted butter
- 1 kaiser roll, halved
- 2 slices peameal bacon (see Note)
- 2 large eggs, whisked
- 1 slice cheddar cheese
- Honey and/or mustard, for serving

1. In a large skillet, melt 1 tablespoon of the butter over medium heat. Add the roll cut-side down and toast until golden, about 4 minutes. Transfer to a plate.
2. Melt 1 more tablespoon butter in the same skillet. Add the bacon and cook until nicely golden, about 2 minutes per side. Stack the bacon on the bottom half of the roll.
3. Melt the final 1 tablespoon butter in the same skillet and pour in the eggs. Fry until almost set, then use a spatula to fold into a square and set the slice of cheese on top. When the cheese begins to melt, transfer the egg square to the top of the bacon.
4. Spread some honey or mustard or both on the top half of the roll before pressing down and serving.

NOTE If you can't find peameal bacon, take a stack of 4 or 5 pieces of Canadian bacon and moisten the outside of the stack. Roll the outside in cornmeal, then refrigerate for 10 minutes to set before frying.

Classic Poutine

Probably the most famous food in Canada, poutine is a beautiful love triangle of french fries, gravy, and cheese curds. (It's honestly shocking that it's not equally famous in the US; we love all those things, too!) The dish originated in Quebec, but my first time eating it was in Toronto, and I immediately wondered where it had been all my life. It's the ultimate late-night snack—salty, rich, and exactly what you need to soak up all those questionable decisions.

FRENCH FRIES

- 2 pounds russet potatoes, unpeeled and scrubbed
- 2 quarts vegetable oil or other neutral oil
- Kosher salt

GRAVY

- 2 tablespoons unsalted butter
- 2 tablespoons all-purpose flour
- 2 cups beef broth
- Kosher salt

- 8 ounces cheese curds (see Note)

1. **Make the french fries:** Cut the potatoes lengthwise into ½-inch-thick ovals, then cut each oval into ½-inch-wide sticks. In a large Dutch oven, combine the potatoes and the oil. Bring the oil to a simmer over high heat, stirring the potatoes often to prevent sticking, about 5 minutes. Cook, stirring occasionally, until the potatoes are nicely browned and crisp, 15 to 20 minutes. Use a slotted spoon to transfer them to paper towels to drain and immediately sprinkle with salt.

2. **Meanwhile, make the gravy:** In a medium saucepan, melt the butter over medium heat. Add the flour and whisk until golden and toasty, about 2 minutes. Slowly pour in the broth a little bit at a time, whisking continuously to avoid lumps. Simmer, whisking occasionally, until slightly thickened, about 4 minutes. Taste and adjust the seasoning. Remove from the heat and cover to keep warm. If needed, rewarm over low heat just before serving.

3. To assemble the poutine, divide the fries between two serving bowls. Spoon a ladleful of gravy over the fries and toss to coat. Divide the cheese curds between the bowls, spoon another ladleful of gravy over the tops, and serve immediately.

NOTE If you can't find cheese curds, substitute with cubed mild cheddar cheese or mozzarella pearls, or a mix of both.

Maple Shortbread Cookies

The first time I tasted *real* maple syrup—like, straight from the Canadian trees—was when my family and I were visiting Niagara Falls in Ontario. I quickly learned that maple-*flavored* syrup had been lying to me my entire life. There were tons of stands with maple snacks and treats all over the town, and I went straight for the maple shortbread. I loved the buttery cookie with the sweet maple icing. It was a match made in heaven. When I'm in the mood to bake, these are the cookies I want every time.

COOKIES

1½ cups (3 sticks) unsalted butter, at room temperature

1 cup granulated sugar

1 tablespoon maple extract

3¼ cups all-purpose flour, plus more as needed

½ teaspoon kosher salt

ICING

4 cups powdered sugar

½ cup pure maple syrup, plus more as needed

Kosher salt

1 **Make the cookies:** In the bowl of a stand mixer fitted with the paddle attachment (or in a large bowl using a handheld mixer), combine the butter and sugar. Beat, starting on low speed and increasing to high, stopping to scrape down the sides as needed, until the mixture is light and fluffy, about 6 minutes. Add the maple extract, flour, and salt, and beat on low until just combined into a cohesive dough. Tightly wrap the dough in plastic wrap and press into a disc. Refrigerate for 30 minutes.

2 Meanwhile, preheat the oven to 350°F. Line 2 rimmed baking sheets with parchment paper.

3 Lightly dust a work surface with flour. Cut the dough into four equal pieces. Work with one piece at a time and keep the rest wrapped in the refrigerator. Dust the top of the dough with flour, then use a rolling pin to roll to a ¼-inch thickness, adding more flour to the surface or dough as needed. Use a maple leaf cookie cutter, or any 4-inch cutter, to cut out 6 cookies. Transfer to one of the prepared baking sheets, spacing the cookies apart evenly. Bake for 15 to 20 minutes, until the edges are just starting to brown. Transfer the cookies to a wire rack to cool completely. While one batch is baking, prepare the next batch.

Recipe continues

4 **When the cookies are cool, make the icing:** In a medium bowl, whisk together the powdered sugar, maple syrup, and a pinch of salt. If necessary, continue adding maple syrup 1 tablespoon at a time until the icing is slightly runny but still thick. Transfer to a piping bag fitted with a small tip (or to a zip-top bag; snip a small corner off the bag before icing).

5 Pipe around the edge of the cookie first, then fill in the center, using a toothpick to smooth over any small gaps. Return the cookies to the wire rack for the icing to set for about 30 minutes before serving. Any leftover cookies can be stored in an airtight container at room temperature for up to 3 days.

Birria Tortas

Birria is a signature of the western Mexican states: a dish of slowly simmered meat in a rich and flavorful consomé, found everywhere from weddings to street carts. I think if you're going to make birria, you should really go big or go home. Personally, I pick the secret third option: Go to a Mexican grocery. I buy bags of dried chiles, make my own sauce from scratch, and cook enough meat to last for days. It can be served as a stew or packed into a taco, but my favorite way to enjoy it is loaded into a torta, with a flavorful consomé for soaking the bread, plus more on the side for dipping. Sometimes I'll even be nice and invite friends over, because birria this good deserves an audience!

1 Preheat the oven to 300°F.

2 **Make the birria:** In a large Dutch oven, heat the vegetable oil over medium heat until it shimmers. Add the chuck roast and a big pinch of salt and cook, turning occasionally, until browned on all sides, about 8 minutes. Remove the beef to a plate, leaving the oil in the pot.

3 Add the chiles, cinnamon, bay leaves, coriander seeds, peppercorns, onions, garlic, and another pinch of salt to the pot. Cook, stirring often, until fragrant, about 2 minutes. Add the tomato paste and cook, stirring, until deep red and fragrant, about 2 minutes, then add the oregano and beef broth. Stir to combine everything, then return the beef to the pot along with any collected juices.

4 Cover the pot and transfer to the oven to roast for 2 to 3 hours, until the beef is falling apart. Check periodically to stir the liquid and add a splash of water if it looks too dry.

5 Transfer the beef to a plate. Using an immersion blender, mix the liquid in the pot on high until a smooth consome forms, about 1 minute. (Or very carefully pour the liquid into a blender, working in batches if necessary, and blend on high until a smooth consomé forms, then pour the consomé back into the pot.) Use two forks to shred the beef, then stir it into the consomé to coat fully. Set the pot over low heat to keep warm.

Recipe and ingredients continue

BIRRIA (See Note)

- 2 tablespoons vegetable oil or other neutral oil
- 2 pounds boneless beef chuck roast
- Kosher salt
- 2 ancho chiles, stemmed and seeded
- 2 guajillo chiles, stemmed and seeded
- 2 chiles de árbol, stemmed and seeded
- 1 cinnamon stick
- 2 bay leaves
- 1 teaspoon dried coriander seeds
- 1 teaspoon whole black peppercorns
- 1 large white onion, diced
- 4 garlic cloves, minced
- 1 tablespoon tomato paste
- 1 teaspoon dried oregano
- 4 cups beef broth

6 **Make the tortas:** Preheat the oven to 250°F. Line a rimmed baking sheet with aluminum foil and set it in the oven to preheat.

7 Place a medium nonstick skillet over medium heat. While the birria rests, a layer of fat will rise to the top. Working with one roll at a time, dip each half into the fat, coating them on both sides. Transfer the two halves, cut-side down, to the warm skillet. Cook until nicely browned, about 2 minutes, then flip so the cut sides face up. Immediately lay some of the Oaxacan cheese on both halves. Cover the skillet until the cheese is melted, 2 to 3 minutes, then transfer the roll to the baking sheet in the oven to stay warm while heating the rest.

8 Remove the baking sheet from the oven. Use tongs to pile some of the beef on the bottom of each roll, then arrange avocado slices on top, add a sprinkle of onions and cilantro, and pile on some lettuce before pressing down the top. Scoop a ladleful of the warm consomé into four small bowls to serve alongside the sandwiches for dunking.

NOTE If the birria ingredients aren't available, substitute a 10-ounce can of red enchilada sauce mixed with 4 cups of beef broth. If you can't find Oaxacan cheese for the tortas, use fresh mozzarella.

TORTAS

- 4 telera rolls or kaiser rolls, split in half
- 8 ounces Oaxaca cheese, pulled into strings (see Note)

FOR SERVING

- Sliced avocado
- Diced white onions
- Chopped fresh cilantro
- Shredded lettuce

RITOS

Migas

When I was in high school, my friends and I would sometimes have potlucks together. (After all, we lived in the Midwest, where potlucks are one of the most important parts of the culture.) At one of our gatherings, a Mexican friend introduced me to migas. With velvety soft eggs, crunch and corn flavor from the tortillas, a hit of salsa spiciness—it was everything I didn't know I needed in my life. It's one of those perfect home-cooking recipes that is so simple but feels so impressive when it all comes together. All these years later, it's still my favorite breakfast trick when I want to serve up something fast and flavorful.

- 2 tablespoons vegetable oil or other neutral oil
- ½ medium white onion, diced
- 2 jalapeños, seeded and diced
- 8 large eggs
- ¼ teaspoon kosher salt
- ¼ teaspoon ground cumin
- 1 cup crushed tortilla chips

FOR SERVING

- Diced avocado
- Chopped fresh cilantro
- Crema or sour cream
- Hot sauce

1. In a medium skillet, heat the vegetable oil over medium heat until it shimmers. Add the onions and jalapeños and cook, stirring occasionally, until the onions begin to soften, about 2 minutes.

2. Meanwhile, in a medium bowl, whisk together the eggs, salt, and cumin. Pour the mixture into the skillet. Sprinkle the crushed chips over the top, then use a rubber spatula to combine the ingredients and scramble the eggs until set, about 3 minutes.

3. Transfer the migas to a serving platter. Top with avocado and cilantro plus a drizzle of crema and a few dashes of hot sauce before serving.

Caramelized Cheese Tacos

I'm usually suspicious about viral food trends, especially the trend of tacos—piled high with ingredients, drenched in sauce, or dripping with cheese—that look like they need an instruction manual to eat. But I saw these caramelized cheese tacos at a Mexican taco truck near my house in LA and was curious. Then I was impressed! They're so easy to make: It's just a simple layer of shredded cheese that melts and browns in a skillet, with a tortilla layered on top hugging the cheese tight like long-lost lovers, and then you have a taco shell that's ready for any filling. Internet trends can keep their sauce-soaked divas—I'll take these salty, caramelized, crunchy queens any day.

¼ cup shredded cheese, such as Monterey Jack, pepper Jack, or cheddar Jack

2 (6-inch) corn tortillas

Migas (page 53), Birria (see page 49), or any other fillings of your choice

1. Heat a large nonstick skillet over medium heat for 2 minutes. Sprinkle the cheese into two small piles in the skillet, dividing evenly. When the cheese is melted and bubbling, 1 to 2 minutes, lay a tortilla on top of each pile, covering about half of the cheese.

2. Use a spatula to press down on the edges of the tortillas to adhere. Cook until the cheese is beginning to crisp on the edges, about 1 minute more, then flip the tortillas.

3. Cook the bottom side just to warm through, about 1 minute, then transfer to a plate. Fill the tortillas with any leftover or fresh fillings before serving.

Elote Corn Ribs

I love elote—Mexican street corn that's grilled, slathered in mayo and lime juice, and garnished with chile powder, Cotija, and lime zest—but it's so messy to eat. These mini corn ribs have all the satisfying flavors of elote, but they're easy for you to eat and still feel like a lady. (Plus, they bake in the oven, so you're not sweating off your contour while babysitting a grill.) I especially love them as an easy party appetizer to pass around, and since they're so simple to make, you can multiply the recipe by as much as you want.

4 ears of corn, shucked

2 tablespoons vegetable oil or other neutral oil

½ cup mayonnaise

½ cup Cotija cheese, crumbled

¼ cup chopped fresh cilantro

Lime wedges

Chile powder

1. Set the broiler to high.
2. Microwave the corn cobs to soften the cores, about 2 minutes. Let cool for about 5 minutes, until cool enough to handle. Cut each cob in half crosswise, then in half again lengthwise. Then cut each piece in half lengthwise one more time to make 8 strips from each cob.
3. Place the strips on a rimmed baking sheet and toss to coat with the vegetable oil, then arrange in a single layer. Broil until nicely charred on both sides, flipping halfway through, about 6 minutes total. Let cool slightly.
4. Brush each rib with mayo and top with a sprinkle of Cotija and cilantro. Add a squeeze of lime and dusting of chile powder before stacking on a serving platter. Serve warm.

Mango Chamoy Paletas

When I lived in Chicago, I was lucky to be around a lot of great Mexican businesses, and my favorites were the ones that sold paletas, Mexican ice pops. On hot Chicago nights (I know that sounds like an oxymoron, but it's real), I would walk to my local paletas shop with the goal of trying a new flavor every time. But the one I kept going back to over and over was mango chamoy. The mix of sweet, creamy mango with tangy, salty, spicy chamoy sauce is a refreshing combo that's more addictive than scrolling on TikTok. These paletas are so easy to whip up and freeze at home, you won't ever have to leave the AC again. For my version, I like to sprinkle the finished paletas with Tajín for an extra little zesty kick!

- 1 (16-ounce) bag frozen mango, thawed
- ⅓ cup sugar
- ¼ cup lime juice (from 3 to 4 limes)
- Chamoy sauce
- Tajín seasoning, for serving

1. In a blender, combine the mango, sugar, and lime juice. Blend on high until smooth, about 2 minutes.
2. In a set of 6 ice pop molds (see Note), place 1 teaspoon chamoy in the bottom of each. Fill halfway with the mango puree, then add another teaspoon chamoy. Fill almost to the top with more puree, then finish with 1 more teaspoon chamoy. Set the sticks in the mold and freeze overnight.
3. When ready to serve, run the molds under warm water to help release the paletas. Dip the top third of each paleta in a glass of cold water, then sprinkle on some Tajín before serving.

NOTE If you don't have ice pop molds, use 8-ounce paper or plastic cups, filled about halfway. Freeze for about 2 hours, until semi-firm, then insert wooden sticks before freezing overnight.

SOUTH AMERICA

In Queso Emergency

If I can count on anything from South America, it's big emotions and even bigger drama. I have vivid memories of my time on tour there, and they're mostly all wild: corrupt police detaining us on the road; a queen and a backup dancer screaming at each other in an airport after partying all night; crowds swarming our bus after a show, making it shake like a carnival ride. Let's just say South America doesn't do boring!

But South American fans are also the sweetest and most passionate in the world. When we landed in Peru, over one hundred fans were waiting at the airport, screaming our names and waving handmade signs. I'd never had that kind of welcome before (or since)! In Argentina, I casually posted on Instagram about a caramel candy I loved, and at the meet-and-greet that night, every single person brought me a box. I had to buy a whole extra suitcase just to haul my candy stash home.

One of my favorite things to look back on is a night in Brazil. I asked a promoter for a local restaurant recommendation, and instead of pulling out Google Maps, she invited me to a barbecue at her house. It's the only time on tour I've felt that kind of genuine love expressed through food, with a side of unmatched hospitality. South America really knows how to serve—on and off the plate.

Hearts of Palm Vegan Ceviche

Ceviche is such a strong part of Peruvian cuisine that UNESCO even put it on the country's list of Intangible Cultural Heritage of Humanity. When I'm in Peru, I eat ceviche pretty much every day. I just can't get enough of the fresh, acidic flavors. It's great lunch fare, perfect as an appetizer, or even as a light dinner entrée. Depending where you live, raw fish can be difficult to source and handle at home. Hearts of palm (probably my favorite canned vegetable of all time) are a perfect substitute, with the same bite, same freshness, and zero raw-fish anxiety.

- 1 (14.1-ounce) can whole hearts of palm, drained, rinsed, and cut into ¼-inch-thick rounds
- ½ medium red onion, thinly sliced
- ½ English cucumber, diced
- 1 beefsteak tomato, diced
- 1 Fresno chile, stemmed, seeded, and thinly sliced
- Juice of 2 limes
- Kosher salt
- ¼ cup finely chopped fresh cilantro
- Plantain chips or tortilla chips, for serving

1. In a medium bowl, toss the hearts of palm with the red onion, cucumber, tomato, chile pepper, lime juice, and a good pinch of salt. Cover the bowl tightly with plastic wrap and let marinate in the refrigerator for at least 1 hour and up to 3 days.
2. Just before serving, add the cilantro to the bowl and toss to mix well. Serve cold with plantain chips.

Lomo Saltado

The first time I went to Peru, I asked the locals what they would consider their country's signature dish—cue every Peruvian shouting "lomo saltado!" They were right: It was everywhere, and I couldn't get enough! The irony is lomo saltado is largely influenced by the Chinese immigrant population in Peru—it's basically a stir-fry using the ingredients that were available to them in their new home. With tender pieces of marinated steak, vegetables blanketed in sauce, and a pile of french fries giving new meaning to the "fry" in "stir-fry," it's one of the most satisfying meals you could possibly make. Like a lot of great food, it's a meeting of two cultures, both influencing each other in all the best ways.

- 2 tablespoons vegetable oil or other neutral oil
- 1 pound sirloin steak, cut into ½-inch-thick strips
- Kosher salt and freshly ground black pepper
- ½ medium red onion, sliced
- 1 beefsteak tomato, cut into wedges
- 4 ají amarillo chiles, or 1 yellow bell pepper, stemmed, seeded, and cut into ½-inch-wide strips
- 2 garlic cloves, minced
- 1 (1-inch) piece fresh ginger, peeled and minced
- 1 tablespoon ají amarillo paste or tomato paste
- 2 tablespoons soy sauce
- 1 tablespoon apple cider vinegar
- 1 tablespoon minced fresh cilantro
- French fries, homemade (see page 43) or store-bought

1. In a large skillet, heat the vegetable oil over medium heat until it shimmers. Add the steak and a good pinch each of salt and pepper. Cook until nicely browned, about 2 minutes per side. Transfer to a plate to rest.

2. To the same skillet, add the onion, tomato, and ají amarillo chiles along with a good pinch of salt. Cook, tossing occasionally, until the vegetables are vibrant in color, about 2 minutes. Stir in the garlic and ginger until fragrant, about 30 seconds, then return the steak to the pan along with any collected juices from the plate.

3. Add the ají amarillo paste, soy sauce, and vinegar and toss to coat everything in the sauce. Quickly simmer to let the flavors combine, about 1 minute, then remove the skillet from the heat and top with the cilantro.

4. Arrange the french fries in an even layer on a serving platter, then pile the stir-fry on top and spoon the sauce over. Serve.

Quinoa Mac and Cheese

Most of the world's supply of the buzzy superfood quinoa comes from Peru, but while traveling there, I found out that Peruvians primarily use it as chicken feed. I am not a chicken, but I do eat a lot of quinoa. Whenever I have a potluck or I'm hosting friends for dinner, I like to make a big batch of this mac and cheese with it. It's hard to resist a dish that's cheesy *and* superfood-adjacent.

Nonstick cooking spray

1 cup black, white, red, or mixed quinoa, rinsed

¼ teaspoon kosher salt, plus more as needed

2 teaspoons vegetable oil or other neutral oil

1 (12-ounce) can evaporated milk

1 tablespoon Dijon mustard

4 ounces low-moisture mozzarella cheese, grated

4 ounces white cheddar cheese, grated

4 ounces queso fresco, crumbled, or Parmesan cheese, grated

2 garlic cloves, grated

1 Place racks in the upper and lower thirds of the oven and preheat to 400°F. Line a baking sheet with parchment paper. Coat an 8-inch-square baking dish with nonstick spray.

2 In a medium saucepan, combine the quinoa, salt, and 1¾ cups water. Bring to a boil over high heat, then cover and reduce the heat to low. Simmer for 15 minutes, then remove the pan from the heat and let sit, still covered, for about 10 minutes, until the quinoa is hydrated and fluffy.

3 Transfer ¼ cup of the quinoa to the prepared baking sheet. Add the vegetable oil, toss to coat, and spread evenly on the baking sheet.

4 In the saucepan, stir the evaporated milk and mustard into the remaining quinoa, then stir in the mozzarella, cheddar, queso fresco, and garlic. Taste and adjust the seasoning. Scrape the mixture into the prepared baking dish.

5 Place the baking sheet on the lower oven rack and the baking dish on the upper rack. Bake together for 20 to 25 minutes, until the quinoa is dark brown and crispy on the baking sheet and the cheese topping is brown and bubbly in the baking dish. Let sit for 10 minutes to set, then sprinkle the crispy quinoa on top of the cheese before serving.

Chimichurri Salmon

In Argentina, I saw chimichurri everywhere—it felt like it was on every table, like we use ketchup in the States. Argentina's love affair with bold, herbal flavors is no secret, so it's no surprise their signature condiment is so vibrant and fresh. Chimichurri is basically a chunky vinaigrette of chopped parsley, garlic, and plenty of olive oil and vinegar that's especially tasty on fatty meats like steak or on, my favorite, simple baked salmon. The herby acidity helps cut through the richness of the fish to make every bite extra delicious.

SALMON

1 (4-pound) skin-on salmon fillet (see Note)

1 tablespoon kosher salt

CHIMICHURRI

1 cup packed fresh parsley leaves, finely chopped

4 garlic cloves, grated

1 teaspoon kosher salt

¼ teaspoon red pepper flakes

¾ cup extra-virgin olive oil

½ cup red wine vinegar

1. **Make the salmon:** Pat the salmon dry with paper towels. Line a baking sheet with parchment paper and set the salmon on top, skin-side down. Sprinkle the salt evenly over the flesh and refrigerate for at least 1 hour and up to 4 hours.
2. When you're ready to bake the salmon, preheat the oven to 450°F.
3. **Make the chimichurri:** In a medium bowl, whisk together the parsley, garlic, salt, red pepper flakes, olive oil, and vinegar.
4. Bake the salmon, straight from the refrigerator, for 12 to 15 minutes, until cooked through. Immediately spoon half of the chimichurri over the salmon and let it rest for 5 minutes to allow the flavors to absorb.
5. Transfer the remaining chimichurri to a small bowl and serve alongside the salmon.

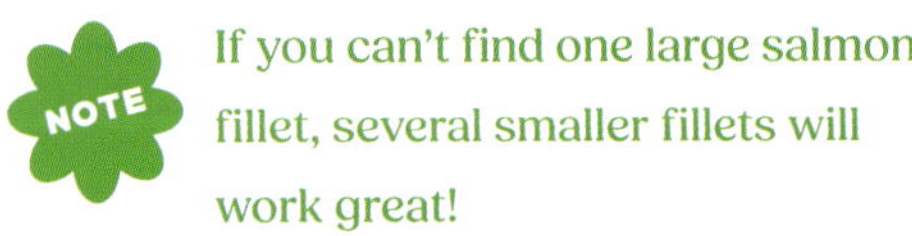

If you can't find one large salmon fillet, several smaller fillets will work great!

Ham and Cheese Empanadas

I would consider empanadas to be the dumplings of Argentina. They're sold everywhere, from convenience stores to restaurants. My personal favorite is the ham and cheese (who doesn't love this combination?!) wrapped in a soft, flaky crust. Empanada dough is pretty easy to make yourself, but a lot of grocery stores sell frozen empanada wrappers (or premade pie dough will work too!) if you want to take a shortcut. I get it; sometimes you just need to stuff cheese in a crust and call it a day.

DOUGH

- 4 tablespoons (½ stick) unsalted butter, melted
- 2 teaspoons apple cider vinegar
- 1½ teaspoons kosher salt
- 3 cups all-purpose flour, plus more for dusting

FILLING

- 1 (7-ounce) smoked ham steak, cubed
- 8 ounces pepper Jack or cheddar Jack cheese, cubed
- 1 tablespoon cornstarch

- 2 quarts vegetable oil or other neutral oil, for frying
- Chimichurri (page 70), for serving (optional)

1. **Make the dough:** In a large bowl, whisk together the butter, vinegar, salt, and 1 cup cold water. Add the flour and use a wooden spoon to stir until a shaggy dough forms.

2. Lightly dust a work surface with flour. Turn the dough out and knead until smooth, about 2 minutes. Wrap tightly with plastic wrap and refrigerate for at least 2 hours.

3. **Make the filling:** In a medium bowl, combine the ham and cheese cubes with the cornstarch to coat evenly.

4. Line a baking sheet with parchment paper.

5. Dust the work surface with flour. Remove the dough from the refrigerator and divide it into 4 pieces. Work with one piece at a time, wrapping the others with plastic wrap and refrigerating them. Roll the dough piece into a 6 by 18-inch rectangle and cut it into three 5-inch rounds. (A small bowl is the perfect size to guide a knife.)

Recipe continues

6. Place 2 tablespoons of the filling in the center of each round, then brush the rim with water. Fold the round in half to create a half-moon and press the edges together. Use a fork to seal the edges or fold into a crimp pattern. Transfer the empanadas to the prepared baking sheet and continue rolling and filling the rest of the dough. Refrigerate the assembled empanadas for 30 minutes.

7. In a Dutch oven or large saucepan, heat the oil over medium heat until it registers 350°F on an instant-read thermometer, or dip the corner of an empanada into the oil to test. It should start bubbling immediately. Working in batches of three, add the empanadas and cook, flipping occasionally, until golden brown all over, about 6 minutes. Repeat with the remaining empanadas, allowing the oil to return to temperature between batches. Transfer to paper towels to drain. Serve hot with chimichurri alongside for dipping, if you like.

Rice and Beef Stuffed Peppers

Argentina is beef heaven—and I'm not just talking about the men. Their cattle are raised with care, their beef is incredibly affordable, and the taste is unreal. I ate stuffed peppers the first night I was in Argentina and was blown away that such a simple dish could be so flavorful. You can make it work with whatever ground beef meets your price point at the grocery store; the layers of seasoning will do all the work here. Plus, eating out of a pepper, my favorite edible bowl, saves you from washing extra dishes.

RED PEPPER SAUCE

2 (16-ounce) jars roasted red peppers, drained

½ cup heavy cream

2 garlic cloves

½ teaspoon kosher salt

STUFFING

½ cup long-grain white rice, rinsed

Kosher salt

4 bell peppers, any color

1 tablespoon extra-virgin olive oil

1 medium white onion, finely diced

1 medium carrot, finely diced

1 celery stalk, finely diced

1 pound ground beef, preferably 80/20

Nonstick cooking spray

1. **Make the red pepper sauce:** In a blender, combine the red peppers, heavy cream, garlic, and salt. Blend on high speed until smooth, about 1 minute.
2. **Make the stuffing:** Preheat the oven to 400°F.
3. In a small saucepan, combine the rice, a big pinch of salt, 2 tablespoons of the red pepper sauce, and 1 cup water. Bring to a boil over high heat. Cover and reduce the heat to low. Simmer for 15 minutes, then remove the pan from the heat and let sit, covered, for about 10 minutes, until the rice is hydrated and fluffy.
4. Lay each bell pepper on its side and slice off the top and stem. Scoop out the seeds and ribs, then turn upright. Discard the stems and finely dice the pepper tops.
5. In a large skillet, heat the olive oil over medium heat until it shimmers. Add the diced pepper tops, onions, carrots, celery, and a good pinch of salt. Cook, stirring occasionally, until the vegetables are vibrant in color, about 2 minutes, then add the ground beef. Cook, using a wooden spoon to break up the beef, until the meat is cooked through, about 5 minutes. Remove the skillet from the heat and stir in the cooked rice. Taste and adjust the seasoning.

Recipe continues

6 Set the peppers in an 8-inch-square baking dish. Fill each cavity with stuffing, packing it tightly and letting some mound on the top. Pour ¾ cup water into the bottom of the baking dish. Coat a piece of aluminum foil with nonstick spray, then cover the baking dish tightly with the foil, coated-side down.

7 Bake for 30 to 40 minutes, until the peppers are fork-tender. Carefully remove the foil (there will be a lot of hot steam).

8 Pour about half of the reserved red pepper sauce on a serving platter or spoon onto individual plates. Set the peppers on top of the sauce, then drizzle the rest of the sauce on top. Serve immediately.

Beef Stroganoff

Beef stroganoff originated in Russia, but lots of countries like Sweden, Australia, Japan, and of course the United States have their own versions. When I was visiting Brazil for a gig, I asked a local what his favorite national dish was, and he said, "You can find beef stroganoff everywhere in this country; it's like our bread and butter." It took me by surprise because I had been thinking of it as such a Midwestern dish! But the Brazilian version has a strong tomato flavor built from savory tomato paste and sweet ketchup, and it's served over rice with crunchy potato sticks on top. Sorry to the Midwest—I'm with Brazil on this one.

- 1 tablespoon vegetable oil or other neutral oil
- 1 pound beef tenderloin or sirloin, cut into 1½-inch cubes
- Kosher salt and freshly ground black pepper
- 1 medium white onion, diced
- 8 ounces white mushrooms, sliced
- 2 garlic cloves, minced
- 1 (6-ounce) can or (4-ounce) tube tomato paste
- 2 tablespoons ketchup
- 2 tablespoons Worcestershire sauce
- 2 cups sour cream
- Cooked white rice (see page 175), for serving
- Potato sticks, for serving

1. In a large skillet, heat the vegetable oil over medium heat until it shimmers. Add the beef and a good pinch each of salt and pepper. Cook until nicely browned, about 2 minutes per side. Transfer to a plate to rest.
2. In the same skillet (no need to wipe it out), combine the onion, mushrooms, and a good pinch each of salt and pepper. Cook over medium heat, scraping up any browned bits from the bottom of the skillet, until the onions are soft and the mushrooms are beginning to brown, about 6 minutes. Stir in the garlic until fragrant, about 30 seconds, then add the beef along with any collected juices from the plate.
3. Add the tomato paste and cook, stirring, until deep red, about 2 minutes, then add the ketchup and Worcestershire sauce. Add ¼ cup water and stir to combine. Bring to a simmer, then stir in the sour cream. Heat until just beginning to simmer again. Remove from the heat and taste and adjust the seasoning.
4. Serve over white rice and topped with potato sticks.

Pão de Queijo

The first time I tried pão de queijo was in seventh grade. I was born in the United States, but when I was five, my family moved to Korea. When we moved back to Michigan, I was in seventh grade, and I had to enroll in ESL to relearn English. The class was full of students from all around the world, so our teacher decided to hold a potluck in which we each brought a dish from our home country. My classmate Marcella from Brazil showed up with a giant bucket filled with round, golden pão de queijo, Brazilian cheese bread. It was love at first bite! The outside had a nice crispness, and the inside was cheesy and a little chewy, kind of like mochi. When I found out how easy they are to make at home, I fell even more in love. Whenever I make this, I swap in different cheeses for a new flavor and new texture each time.

MAKES 24 PÃO DE QUEIJO

- Nonstick cooking spray
- 2/3 cup whole milk
- 1/3 cup vegetable oil or other neutral oil
- 1 large egg
- 1 1/2 cups tapioca flour or tapioca starch
- 1/2 cup grated cheese of your choice, such as cheddar, mozzarella, Parmesan, or a mixture
- 1/2 teaspoon kosher salt

1. Preheat the oven to 400°F. Coat a 24-cup mini muffin tin with nonstick spray.
2. In a blender or food processor, combine the milk, vegetable oil, egg, tapioca flour, cheese, and salt. Blend until smooth, about 1 minute. (This can also be done in a large bowl with a whisk, but it will take longer.)
3. Pour the batter into the prepared muffin tin, leaving about 1/4 inch at the top of each cup. Bake for 15 to 20 minutes, until golden brown. Remove the pão de queijo to a wire rack to cool.
4. Serve the pão de queijo warm or at room temperature. Store any leftovers in an airtight container at room temperature for up to 3 days.

Brigadeiro Cake

Brigadeiros are Brazil's version of chocolate truffles, and they're perfect. A soft chocolate ball, dark and bitter and covered in sprinkles, is such a fun little treat. I've only ever had it in this form, and it's over in a couple bites. So in true American fashion, I decided to supersize it into a cake! But really, it's just an excuse to enjoy a rich chocolate cake, slathered in frosting, blanketed in sprinkles, and crowned with a ring of brigadeiros like it just won a pageant. It lasts way more than a couple bites, and that's what matters!

BRIGADEIROS

- 1 (14-ounce) can sweetened condensed milk
- 6 tablespoons unsweetened cocoa powder
- 1 tablespoon unsalted butter
- Kosher salt
- 1 cup chocolate sprinkles

CAKE

- Nonstick cooking spray
- ¾ cup (1½ sticks) unsalted butter, at room temperature
- 2 cups granulated sugar
- 4 large eggs
- ½ cup unsweetened cocoa powder
- ½ cup boiling water
- 2 cups all-purpose flour
- 2 teaspoons baking soda
- 1 teaspoon kosher salt
- 1 cup buttermilk
- 2 teaspoons pure vanilla extract

1. **Make the brigadeiros:** In a medium skillet, whisk together the condensed milk and cocoa powder until smooth. Add the butter and a pinch of salt and set over medium heat. Cook, stirring continuously with a spatula, until the mixture thickens and pulls together, 10 to 12 minutes. Remove the skillet from the heat.

2. Cover a large plate with parchment paper and scrape the chocolate mixture on top. Refrigerate for 30 minutes until cool.

3. Place the sprinkles in a small bowl. Scoop the cooled chocolate mixture into six 2-inch balls, about 2 tablespoons each, and roll through the sprinkles to coat all over. Arrange the balls on a clean plate and cover with aluminum foil. Return to the refrigerator until ready to use, up to 5 days.

4. **Make the cake:** Preheat the oven to 350°F. Line the bottom of two 9-inch cake pans with parchment paper rounds and coat the rounds and sides with nonstick spray.

5. In the bowl of a stand mixer fitted with the paddle attachment (or in a large bowl with a handheld mixer), beat the butter and granulated sugar together on medium speed until light and airy, about 4 minutes. Scrape down the sides of the bowl and add the eggs one at a time, fully incorporating each before adding the next. Scrape down the sides again.

Recipe and ingredients continue

6 In a separate small bowl, whisk together the cocoa powder and boiling water. Scrape the mixture into the stand mixer bowl and beat on low speed until combined. Add the flour, baking soda, and salt and beat on low until almost combined. Add the buttermilk and vanilla and beat on low again until just combined. Scrape the sides and bottom of the bowl to be sure all ingredients have been incorporated. Divide the batter between the prepared pans.

7 Bake for 25 to 30 minutes, rotating the pans halfway through, until a toothpick inserted into the centers comes out clean. Let the cakes cool completely in the pans, about 2 hours.

8 **Make the frosting:** In the bowl of a stand mixer fitted with the whisk attachment (or in a large bowl with a handheld mixer), beat the butter and cream cheese on medium speed until light and airy, about 4 minutes. Scrape down the sides of the bowl and add the powdered sugar and cocoa powder. Beat again on low until combined. Add the melted chocolate and sour cream and beat on high until combined and fluffy. The frosting can be used immediately or transferred to an airtight container and refrigerated for up to 5 days (bring to room temperature before using).

9 To assemble the cake, remove the cakes from the pans and discard the parchment. Use a serrated knife to slice the domed tops off for a flat surface on each cake. In the center of a cake stand or serving plate, add a dollop of frosting. Flip one cake upside down and center it over the frosting. Cut a piece of parchment into 4 strips and slide them under the bottom edge of the cake to keep the surface clean while frosting.

10 Scoop about 1½ cups of frosting over the top. Flip the other cake upside down and set over the frosting. Spread about 1 cup of frosting in a thin layer over the top and sides of the cake. Refrigerate to set, about 15 minutes.

11 Set aside 2 tablespoons of the frosting and spread the remaining frosting evenly over the top and sides of the cake. Pour some sprinkles into the palm of your hand. Starting at the bottom of the cake, quickly tip your palm and run it up the side toward the top to spread sprinkles on the side. Continue rotating the cake and applying sprinkles in batches along the side, then spread sprinkles evenly over the top. Chill for about 30 minutes to set completely. Remove the parchment strips and brush away any stray sprinkles. Spread a small dollop of the reserved frosting on the bottom of each brigadeiro and stick them to the top of the cake. Serve immediately.

FROSTING

¾ cup (1½ sticks) unsalted butter, at room temperature

1 (8-ounce) package cream cheese, at room temperature

2½ cups powdered sugar

½ cup unsweetened cocoa powder

8 ounces semisweet chocolate, melted and cooled

½ cup sour cream

2 cups chocolate sprinkles

EUROPE

Eat, Pray, Love Handles

Traveling through Europe was on my bucket list, but touring there came with challenges—namely, the catering. My palate didn't want to RSVP to a bland banquet, so I skipped the food provided to us and made it my mission to eat out as much as possible. I went hunting for local gems where an English translation wasn't usually on the menu. I wasn't always given the warmest welcome, but the food was worth the side-eye every time.

This is a long story, but while I was in France, I got to work backstage with the makeup crew for Paris Fashion Week shows. After we wrapped, the crew took me to a grocery store, where we loaded up on cheese, fruit, and charcuterie, and then proceeded to have a picnic right in front of the Eiffel Tower. Was I in a movie? I felt très chic.

The real magic of Europe is how it forces you to slow down. Meals are an event, meant to be shared around the table with loved ones, never a rush job. You have room to breathe, enjoy every moment, and savor every bite. They'll never throw the check at you before you've swallowed your last bite!

Of course, the fans were a highlight, too. At a meet-and-greet in Spain, a kid told me, "Valentina makes me proud to be Latino, and you make me proud to be fat." Iconic.

Curry and Chips (Chippy Shop Style)

Brits love to pour curry sauce all over everything, from Chinese food to fried fish. The truth is, I get it: The stuff is *extremely* good. And I say if you can't beat 'em, join 'em. When it's late at night, I love dousing my chippy shop chips (that's British for "french fries") with a pool of curry sauce and going to bed full and satisfied. Luckily, this homemade version of curry and chips saves me a fortune on airfare, and no one's judging if I have it for breakfast, lunch, and dinner.

- 2 tablespoons vegetable oil or other neutral oil
- 1 large white onion, diced
- 2 garlic cloves, minced
- 1 (1-inch) piece fresh ginger, peeled and diced
- 1 teaspoon ground cumin
- 1 teaspoon ground turmeric
- 1 teaspoon curry powder
- 1 teaspoon smoked paprika
- 1 teaspoon ground coriander
- ½ teaspoon kosher salt
- ½ teaspoon freshly ground black pepper
- 2 tablespoons tomato paste
- 1 tablespoon all-purpose flour
- Juice of 1 lemon
- French fries, homemade (page 43) or store-bought

1. In a large saucepan, heat the vegetable oil over medium heat until it shimmers. Add the onions, garlic, and ginger and cook, stirring often, until the onions are translucent, about 8 minutes. Add the cumin, turmeric, curry powder, paprika, coriander, salt, and pepper and cook, stirring, until fragrant, about 30 seconds. Stir in the tomato paste and flour until the paste is a deep red and incorporated, about 3 minutes.
2. Pour in 1½ cups water. Cook, stirring occasionally, until the sauce thickens and reduces slightly, about 10 minutes. Add the lemon juice and, using an immersion blender, blend on high until smooth, about 1 minute. (Or very carefully transfer the mixture to a blender and blend on high until smooth.) Taste and adjust the seasoning.
3. Pile your chips in a large, shallow serving bowl. Pour the curry sauce over the top just to cover the chips, then pour the rest into a small bowl to serve alongside for dipping. Dig in!

NOTE If your spice rack is missing some of those called for here, a good jarred curry blend will get you close enough!

Minty Pea Salad

When I'm in the UK, I sometimes struggle to find good healthy greens, especially as someone who loves vegetables and salads . . . and is spoiled by LA's food scene. Late at night after a gig, the only options are from greasy chip shops, which serve mushy peas: the closest to a green a girl can get. This salad is inspired by the UK's favorite vegetable but gives it a California glow-up that both sides of the pond will love.

- 1 tablespoon kosher salt, plus more to taste
- 1 cup frozen or fresh peas
- 1 cup fresh sugar snap peas, cut on an angle in ½-inch pieces
- 1 cup fresh snow peas, cut on an angle in ½-inch pieces
- 2 cups packed baby arugula
- ¼ cup packed fresh mint leaves
- ¼ cup packed fresh dill fronds
- Juice of 1 lemon
- 1 tablespoon extra-virgin olive oil
- Freshly ground black pepper

1. In a large saucepan, combine the salt with 6 cups water. Bring to a boil over high heat. Meanwhile, fill a large bowl halfway with ice water.
2. Lower the peas, snap peas, and snow peas into the boiling water. Cook until vibrant green, about 2 minutes, then use a slotted spoon to remove and plunge immediately into the ice water. Let cool completely, about 2 minutes, then drain.
3. Meanwhile, in a large bowl, toss the arugula, mint, and dill with the lemon juice, olive oil, and a good pinch each of salt and pepper. Taste and adjust the seasoning. Add the peas to the bowl and toss again, then serve immediately.

Cheese and Onion Cornish Pasties

When I was touring the UK, the tour promoter drove me from city to city in his tiny car, and I ended up discovering the joy of their rest stops. They are heaven, showcasing some combination of a mini-mart, donut shop, KFC, coffee shop, and the country's most popular bakery chain, Greggs. At one stop, I found a local bakery specializing in Cornish pasties, which are like giant empanadas with a buttery and flaky outer shell. The inside is filled with savory ingredients ranging from beef stew, lamb and mint, and stewed veggies to a full English breakfast. The one that stood out to me most was the pasty with cheese and onion filling. It was so comforting, with sweet onion perfectly matched by savory cheese. My recipe here is a simple version using puff pastry for an extra-buttery crunch.

- 1 medium russet potato, peeled and chopped into bite-size pieces
- 1 tablespoon plus 1 teaspoon kosher salt
- 1 tablespoon vegetable oil or other neutral oil
- 2 tablespoons unsalted butter
- 1 large white onion, diced
- 1 tablespoon thyme leaves
- 2 cups grated white cheddar cheese
- 1 large egg
- All-purpose flour, for dusting
- 2 sheets puff pastry (from a 17.3-ounce box), thawed

1. Preheat the oven to 425°F. Line a rimmed baking sheet with parchment paper.
2. In a large saucepan, combine the potatoes, 1 tablespoon of the salt, and 6 cups water. Bring to a boil over high heat, then cook until the potatoes are fork-tender, about 10 minutes. Drain and let cool.
3. Meanwhile, in a large skillet, combine the vegetable oil and butter over medium heat. When the butter is melted, add the onions and thyme. Cook, stirring occasionally, until the onions are soft and translucent, about 8 minutes. Remove from the heat and add the cheese, boiled potatoes, and remaining 1 teaspoon salt. Mash everything together until it's well mixed.
4. In a small bowl, beat the egg with 1 tablespoon water.
5. Lightly dust a work surface with flour. Unfold the sheets of puff pastry onto the surface and use a 3-inch biscuit cutter or the rim of a drinking glass to cut three circles from each sheet. Discard the scraps.

Recipe continues

6 Working with one piece at a time, and adding more flour as needed, roll out each circle to about 6 inches in diameter. Lightly brush the perimeter with the egg wash, then pile about 2 tablespoons of the filling in the center. Fold the circle in half and use a fork to seal the edges together. Place on the prepared baking sheet. Repeat with the remaining dough and filling, spacing apart the filled pasties.

7 Bake for 15 to 20 minutes, until the pasties are puffed and golden. Transfer to a wire rack to cool for about 10 minutes before serving—careful, they'll still be piping hot inside!

Strawberry Mille-Feuilles

I could write a whole book about how much I love French desserts. Thanks to the country's expertise in pastry, its sweets can be intricate and complex, but mille-feuille is one of the few that are easy to make at home—and it still looks impressive! Mille-feuilles are made from crispy, buttery layers of puff pastry with a simple pastry cream as the soft, sweet filling. Usually that's it, but I like to level up with some jammy strawberries—you know, for a little extra glam.

- ½ cup plus 2 tablespoons granulated sugar
- 2 tablespoons cornstarch
- 2 large egg yolks
- ¾ cup whole milk
- 1 teaspoon pure vanilla extract
- 1 tablespoon unsalted butter
- All-purpose flour, for dusting
- 2 sheets puff pastry (from a 17.3-ounce box), thawed
- 1 pound fresh strawberries, quartered
- ¼ cup heavy cream
- Powdered sugar, for serving

1. In a medium bowl, whisk together ½ cup of the granulated sugar and the cornstarch to combine. Add the egg yolks and whisk until smooth.
2. In a medium saucepan, heat the milk over medium heat until it simmers. Pour a couple splashes of the warm milk into the egg mixture, whisking continuously so the eggs don't scramble. Pour the tempered egg mixture into the saucepan over medium heat. Cook, whisking continuously, until the mixture is thick and bubbly, about 3 minutes. Remove from the heat and whisk in the vanilla and butter. Pour the pastry cream through a fine-mesh strainer into another medium bowl. Press plastic wrap directly on the surface of the cream and refrigerate until chilled, at least 2 hours and up to 3 days.
3. Preheat the oven to 425°F. Line two baking sheets with parchment paper.
4. Lightly dust a work surface with flour. Unfold one sheet of puff pastry and roll it into a 12-inch square, then cut it into six 2 by 4-inch rectangles. Arrange the rectangles on one of the prepared baking sheets, spacing them apart, then lay another piece of parchment over the pastry.

Recipe continues

5 On the other prepared baking sheet, toss the strawberries with the remaining 2 tablespoons granulated sugar. Set the baking sheet directly on top of the other, to ensure the puff pastry stays flat.

6 Transfer the double-deck baking sheets to the oven. Bake for 15 minutes, until the strawberries are soft and juicy and the puff pastry is golden brown. Separate the baking sheets and let both cool completely, about 30 minutes. Remove the pastry pieces to a plate. Roll and cut the second sheet of puff pastry in the same manner and repeat the baking process, without the strawberries this time.

7 Meanwhile, uncover the chilled pastry cream and whisk in the heavy cream. Transfer the pastry cream to a piping bag fitted with a small tip (or to a zip-top bag; snip a small corner off the bag before piping).

8 To assemble the mille-feuilles, place one layer of pastry on a plate. Pipe three lines of cream across the width of the pastry. Spoon the strawberry mixture in between the lines, then top with another piece of pastry. Add another layer of cream and fruit, then top with a third piece of pastry. Repeat with the remaining pastry, cream, and strawberry mixture to create four mille-feuilles. Dust the tops with powdered sugar and serve immediately.

Custardy Soft Scrambled Eggs

I love working in Paris, one of the great food capitals of the world. But I also like to eat a hearty breakfast and the French keep it light—usually just a croissant and espresso. The only other option I could find was a soft scrambled egg, which I ordered reluctantly. What a surprise! It feels like eating a buttery, eggy custard with extra fat and protein, but it's a light dish that's actually filling. This gives me all the energy I need to run around the city, whether I'm home in LA or Kimily in Paris.

- 6 large eggs
- ¼ cup whole milk
- ¼ teaspoon kosher salt
- 2 tablespoons unsalted butter
- 1 tablespoon thinly sliced fresh chives
- Freshly ground black pepper
- Warm baguette, for serving

1. In a small saucepan, whisk together the eggs, milk, and salt until smooth. Add the butter and cook over low heat, whisking continuously, until the eggs thicken to a soft scramble with very small curds. Remove from the heat when the eggs are about 75 percent cooked.
2. Add the chives and a few cracks of black pepper. I like my eggs runny, but you can let them sit in the residual heat, stirring occasionally, until they're set to your preference.
3. Serve the eggs immediately with slices of warm baguette.

Lemon Sole

Not to be that girl, but I first had lemon sole while I was sitting on the patio of a bistro in Paris, feeling très chic on a cool fall afternoon. Can't you picture it? I felt even more chic when I got home and made it for myself. Like a lot of French dishes, it's simple—but that means the magic is in the small details and best ingredients. When I don't know what I feel like for dinner, this light and refreshing meal is never the wrong answer.

- 4 (4-ounce) skinless sole fillets
- Kosher salt and freshly ground black pepper
- ½ cup all-purpose flour
- 4 tablespoons unsalted butter
- 1 tablespoon extra-virgin olive oil
- 1 teaspoon fresh thyme leaves
- 1 tablespoon drained capers
- Juice of 1 lemon
- Chopped fresh parsley, for garnish
- Lemon wedges, for serving

1. Pat the fish dry with paper towels and season on both sides with salt and pepper. On a large plate, spread out the flour and dredge each fillet, lightly pressing to adhere the flour and shaking off any excess.
2. In a large skillet, combine the butter and olive oil over medium heat. When the butter is melted, add two fillets to the skillet. Cook for about 3 minutes on each side, until lightly browned and cooked through. Transfer to a serving plate and repeat with the remaining fillets.
3. Add the thyme and capers to the skillet (no need to wipe it out), stirring until the thyme is fragrant, about 1 minute. Add the lemon juice and swirl the skillet to mix it into the butter sauce. When the sauce is bubbling, pour it evenly over the fillets.
4. Garnish the fish with parsley and serve with lemon wedges on the side for squeezing.

Pan con Tomate

I am a tomato fanatic: I love tomato everything and anything. When I first went to Spain, I stumbled upon a pan con tomate station in every hotel lobby. It's a choose-your-own-adventure of thick bread, a bowl of runny grated tomato, and all the olive oil you could want. After watching a few Spaniards turn these three things into a magical snack of pan con tomate, I had to try it for myself. I immediately realized Spanish tomatoes beat all the others I'd ever had. Now when I'm in Spain, I start every morning with a thick pan con tomate. And when I'm back home, I'm always counting down to tomato season like it's Christmas so I can enjoy my favorite light and tangy breakfast.

- 1 very ripe beefsteak tomato
- Kosher salt
- 1/4 cup extra-virgin olive oil, plus more for serving
- 2 thick slices of crusty bread
- 1/2 garlic clove

1. Cut the tomato in half. Set a box grater over a small bowl and run the tomato halves over the large holes, discarding the skin. Season with a good pinch of salt.
2. In a large skillet, heat the olive oil over medium heat until it shimmers. Place the two slices of bread in the skillet. Cook until nicely golden brown, about 4 minutes per side. Transfer to a plate and lightly rub the top of each slice with the garlic clove.
3. Spoon the grated tomato over each piece of toast, then drizzle with olive oil. Serve immediately.

Rice Cooker Paella

While the *Werq the World* tour was in Madrid, the promoter asked what we wanted to eat after the show. I said traditional Spanish food, and he said he would take care of it. When we came off stage, there was a giant pan of paella that his mom had cooked just for us. It was incredible and is still one of my favorite food memories. Since I don't have a traditional paella pan at home, and you probably don't either, I created this rice cooker version (and you will need a medium or large rice cooker for this recipe) that delivers all the flavors with way less effort. Because ain't nobody got time for complicated recipes!

- 1 cup short-grain rice, such as bomba
- 2 cups vegetable broth or chicken broth
- 2 teaspoons smoked paprika
- 2 teaspoons dried oregano
- 1 teaspoon kosher salt
- 2 bay leaves
- ½ yellow onion, diced
- ½ red bell pepper, diced
- ½ green bell pepper, diced
- 2 garlic cloves, minced
- ½ pound Spanish chorizo, sliced
- ½ pound boneless, skinless chicken thighs, cut into bite-size pieces
- 1 (14.5-ounce) can diced tomatoes
- ½ cup frozen peas
- Seafood, for serving (optional; see Note)
- Finely chopped fresh parsley, for serving (optional)

1. In a medium or large rice cooker, combine the rice, broth, paprika, oregano, salt, and bay leaves. Stir to mix the spices into the liquid. Add the onions, bell peppers, garlic, chorizo, and chicken, and pour the tomatoes and their juices over the top.

2. Close the rice cooker and set to the white rice setting. When the cooker finishes, open the lid and use a fork to mix the ingredients and fluff the rice. Add the peas on top and close the lid. Let the paella steam for 10 minutes more.

3. Spoon the paella onto a serving platter. Top with seafood, if using, and finish with parsley, if you like. Serve immediately.

NOTE Calamari, shrimp, and mussels are all traditionally part of a big pan of paella, but they will turn rubbery in the rice cooker. So as soon as my rice is done and the peas are in, I like to quickly steam my seafood separately. Use 1½ pounds of any combination of calamari, cleaned and cut into rings; shrimp, peeled and deveined with the tails on; and/or mussels, scrubbed and debearded (see page 122). In a large pot, bring 1 inch of water to a simmer. Arrange the seafood in a steamer basket or colander and set it in the pot, making sure it's not touching the water. Cover the pot and steam for 5 to 7 minutes, until the seafood is cooked through. Discard any mussels that haven't opened.

Croquetas de Jamón Serrano

I first had these croquetas at a bar in Spain. My friends and I were looking for a snack to pair with our drinks, so I ordered the cheapest thing on the menu (because priorities). When the croquetas arrived, crispy on the outside and creamy on the inside, I was immediately obsessed—and ordered more. When friends are coming over and you need the perfect little snack, these will never do you wrong.

- 4 tablespoons (½ stick) unsalted butter
- ¼ cup extra-virgin olive oil
- 1 medium yellow onion, finely diced
- 8 ounces Serrano ham, diced
- Kosher salt and freshly ground black pepper
- Ground nutmeg
- 1½ cups all-purpose flour
- 4 cups whole milk
- 2 large eggs
- 1 cup panko breadcrumbs
- 4 cups vegetable oil or other neutral oil, for frying

1. In a large saucepan, heat the butter and olive oil over medium heat. When the butter has melted, add the onions, ham, and a pinch each of salt, pepper, and nutmeg. Cook, stirring occasionally, until the onions are soft and translucent, about 8 minutes. Add 1 cup of the flour and cook, stirring continuously, until golden brown, about 2 minutes.
2. Very slowly add the milk a little bit at a time, stirring continuously to avoid lumps. When the milk is fully incorporated, you should have a thick dough. If it's still a little runny, stir until it thickens.
3. Remove from the heat and let cool to room temperature, about 1 hour. Transfer the dough to a medium bowl and smooth into an even layer. Press plastic wrap directly on the surface of the dough and refrigerate overnight until firm.
4. Set a wire rack over a rimmed baking sheet. In a medium bowl, place the remaining ½ cup flour. In a separate medium bowl, beat the eggs with a pinch of salt. In a third medium bowl, spread out the panko.
5. Scoop and shape the dough into 16 equal logs, using about ¼ cup of dough for each. Working with one at a time, roll each log in the flour, then dip into the egg, then coat with the panko, pressing lightly to adhere. Place the breaded logs on the wire rack.

Recipe continues

6. In a Dutch oven or large saucepan, heat the vegetable oil over medium heat until it registers 350°F on an instant-read thermometer, or drop a pinch of panko in the oil to test. It should start bubbling immediately. Working in batches of 3 or 4, drop the croquetas into the oil, flipping them periodically, until golden brown all over, about 5 minutes. Use a slotted spoon to transfer them back to the wire rack to drain. Repeat with the remaining croquetas, allowing the oil to return to temperature between batches.
7. Arrange the croquetas on a plate and serve warm.

NOTE The croquetas will be very hot inside, so it's okay to let them cool a little bit while you finish frying.

Döner Kebab Board

Turkish döner kebabs are everywhere you turn in Berlin, the reigning kings of late-night street food. I fell in love with the bold flavors—juicy meats, crunchy veggies, and that killer white sauce. I love translating a traditional kebab into this shareable board for my friends and family. Perfectly seasoned chicken thighs and lamb kofta get slowly baked in the oven and then spread out with veggies, pita, and the classic white sauce and hot sauce so every person can DIY their ideal plate.

1 Preheat the oven to 350°F.

2 **Make the white sauce:** In a small bowl, whisk together the sour cream, mayonnaise, lemon juice, vinegar, sugar, salt, pepper, and 2 tablespoons cold water. Cover with plastic wrap and refrigerate until ready to use, up to 3 days.

3 **Make the kofta:** In a large bowl, combine the ground lamb, olive oil, onion powder, garlic powder, cumin, paprika, oregano, salt, and pepper. Mix well to season the meat thoroughly. On a work surface, lay down two large pieces of aluminum foil on top of each other. Pile the meat mixture in the center and pat it into a log, then wrap the log tightly with the first layer of foil. Wrap the log tightly with the second layer and place in a 9 by 13-inch baking dish.

4 **Make the chicken:** In the same bowl, combine the chicken, olive oil, onion powder, garlic powder, cumin, turmeric, cinnamon, salt, and pepper. Mix to season well, then repeat the process with two more layers of foil, making a log the same way as the kofta, and nestling the log into the same baking dish.

Recipe and ingredients continue

WHITE SAUCE

½ cup sour cream

½ cup mayonnaise

2 tablespoons fresh lemon juice

1 tablespoon white wine vinegar

1 tablespoon sugar

¼ teaspoon kosher salt

¼ teaspoon freshly ground black pepper

KOFTA

1 pound ground lamb or beef

2 tablespoons extra-virgin olive oil

2 teaspoons onion powder

2 teaspoons garlic powder

2 teaspoons ground cumin

2 teaspoons smoked paprika

2 teaspoons dried oregano

1 teaspoon kosher salt

1 teaspoon freshly ground black pepper

5 Pour water into the dish until it's about halfway up the sides of the logs, then carefully transfer to the oven. Bake for about 1 hour, carefully unwrapping to check the meat is cooked through and tender. Add splashes of water to the baking dish as needed so it doesn't dry out.

6 Let the meat rest for 15 minutes before unwrapping and thinly slicing. Arrange the meat on a serving platter along with pita, lettuce, onions, tomatoes, cucumbers, the bowl of white sauce, and a bowl of hot sauce. Serve immediately.

CHICKEN

- 1 pound boneless, skinless chicken thighs
- 2 tablespoons extra-virgin olive oil
- 2 teaspoons onion powder
- 2 teaspoons garlic powder
- 2 teaspoons ground cumin
- 2 teaspoons ground turmeric
- 1 teaspoon ground cinnamon
- 1 teaspoon kosher salt
- 1 teaspoon freshly ground black pepper

FOR SERVING

- Toasted pita bread, quartered
- Shredded lettuce
- Thinly sliced red onion
- Sliced tomatoes
- Thinly sliced cucumbers
- Hot sauce

German Potato Salad Dip

The first time I had German potato salad was on my way home after the *Werq the World* tour. I got stuck in Hamburg overnight because of a missed connection, so I did what I do best: I went out to eat! I ordered a schnitzel with a side of potato salad—it was so complex, with rich, acidic, and herbal notes all mixed together in every bite. I wanted to adapt those flavors into a creamy potato dip because, let's be honest, people will *always* go back for seconds if it's in dip form. No polite portions here—you're going to need extra chips to fend off the competition.

- ½ pound red baby potatoes, halved
- 2 teaspoons kosher salt, plus more as needed
- 2 slices bacon
- 1 small shallot, diced
- 1 (8-ounce) package cream cheese, at room temperature
- 2 tablespoons whole milk
- 1 tablespoon chopped fresh dill
- 1 tablespoon spicy brown mustard
- 1 scallion, thinly sliced
- Kettle chips, for serving

1. In a large saucepan, combine the potatoes, 4 cups water, and the salt. Bring to a boil over high heat. Cook until the potatoes are fork-tender, about 10 minutes. Drain.

2. In a large skillet, cook the bacon over medium heat, until the fat has rendered and the bacon is crisp, 6 to 8 minutes. Use tongs to transfer the bacon to paper towels to drain.

3. To the bacon fat in the skillet, add the shallots. Cook over medium heat, stirring with a wooden spoon, until the shallots are softened, about 2 minutes. Add the potatoes and toss to coat. Use the spoon to mash the potatoes until mostly broken down but with a little bit of texture left. Remove from the heat and stir in the cream cheese to melt. Stir in the milk, dill, and mustard.

4. Transfer the dip to a serving bowl. Break the bacon into pieces and sprinkle on top of the dip along with the scallions. Serve immediately with kettle chips for dipping.

Schnitzel Sandos

My favorite food to eat in Germany is schnitzel, not just because it's amazing, but because it's the OG ancestor of Korean donkatsu: fried pork cutlet. Since everything is better as a sandwich, I love eating my schnitzel on a pretzel roll (thanks again, Germany!), slathered with lemon-dill mayo and piled high with tangy sauerkraut to cut through all that richness.

- ½ cup mayonnaise
- 2 tablespoons fresh lemon juice
- 2 teaspoons chopped fresh dill
- ½ cup all-purpose flour
- 1 large egg
- 1 cup panko breadcrumbs
- 2 (8-ounce) boneless pork chops
- Kosher salt and freshly ground black pepper
- ½ cup vegetable oil, plus more as needed
- 2 pretzel rolls
- Sauerkraut and baby arugula, for serving

1. In a small bowl, whisk together the mayonnaise, lemon juice, and dill. Cover with plastic wrap and refrigerate until ready to use.
2. On a large plate, spread out the flour. On a separate large, deep plate, whisk the egg. On a third large plate, spread out the panko.
3. On a cutting board, place the pork chops between two sheets of plastic wrap. Use a meat mallet or rolling pin to pound each pork chop to about a ¼-inch thickness. Season on both sides with salt and pepper. Dredge each pork chop in the flour, then dip into the egg, then coat with panko, pressing lightly to adhere. Return to the cutting board to rest.
4. In a medium skillet, heat the oil over medium heat until it shimmers. Working one at a time, add a cutlet and cook until golden brown, about 4 minutes per side. Transfer to a clean plate and season with a pinch of salt. Add more oil to the skillet if needed before cooking the second cutlet.
5. To assemble the sandwiches, spread the lemon-dill mayo inside each half of the rolls. Set the cutlets on the bottom halves of each, then pile on the sauerkraut and arugula. Press the tops of the rolls on to close and serve immediately.

Bag Frites with Endless Aioli

Belgium is one of the most beautiful places to sightsee. It's even more beautiful when you're walking around with a paper cone loaded with thick-cut fries and a mountain of aioli. When I'm back home, this is one of my favorite things to share with friends, spread out on a repurposed paper bag with aioli on the side for dunking. I haven't quite figured out how to pack this to go while driving in my car, but as soon as I do, I'll be unstoppable.

- 1 tablespoon fresh lemon juice
- 1 tablespoon minced red onion
- 1 tablespoon minced green bell pepper
- 1 tablespoon minced red bell pepper
- ¼ teaspoon kosher salt
- 1 cup mayonnaise
- 2 tablespoons tomato paste
- French fries, homemade (page 43) or store-bought
- Chopped fresh parsley, for serving

1. In a small bowl, combine the lemon juice, red onions, bell peppers, and salt and toss to coat. Let sit for 5 minutes to marinate. Add the mayonnaise and tomato paste and whisk until smooth.
2. Spread the hot fries directly on a paper bag and sprinkle fresh parsley on top. Set the bowl of aioli alongside and let everyone do their thing.

Belgian Beer Mussels

One of the main reasons I decided to move to Chicago was mussels. In high school, my class took a field trip to Chicago, and while walking around during some downtime, I passed a woman sitting outside a restaurant, eating a bowl of mussels. She was so glamorous—I knew I wanted to be her one day. I had only ever had mussels steamed with wine until I went to Belgium and had them made with beer for the first time. The hoppy flavor of Belgian ale is a perfect match for the slightly sweet, salty flavor of the mussels, but this recipe can be made with the same amount of white wine instead if you prefer. Either way, this is the ultimate chic date food, perfect to pair with drinks and to feel glamorous together.

- 2 pounds mussels, scrubbed and debearded (see Note)
- 1 large shallot, diced
- 2 garlic cloves, minced
- 8 sprigs fresh thyme
- 1 cup Chimay or Belgian ale
- Kosher salt and freshly ground black pepper
- 2 tablespoons unsalted butter
- Crusty bread, for serving

1. In a large Dutch oven, combine the mussels, shallots, garlic, thyme, ale, and a good pinch each of salt and pepper. Cover and bring to a boil over high heat until the mussels begin to open, about 5 minutes. Use tongs to remove any fully open mussels to a serving bowl. Cover the pot again, give it a good shake, and steam the remaining mussels for 5 minutes more, checking periodically to transfer open ones to the bowl. Discard any mussels that have not opened by the end of the cook time.
2. When all the mussels have been transferred, remove the pot from the heat. Add the butter to the pot and stir until melted. Taste and adjust the seasoning, then pour the sauce over the mussels.
3. Serve immediately with plenty of crusty bread alongside for dipping.

NOTE To clean the mussels, run the shells under cold water and scrub with a brush or the rough side of a sponge to remove any dirt and debris. Next, locate the fibrous strands (the beard!) near the hinge of the shell. Pinch the beard, pull it toward the tip of the shell, and rip it out and discard it.

Lotus

WHIP
EGG WHITES
CREAM
FROSTINGS
CANDIES
VEGETABLES
MIX
CAKE
PUDDINGS
BATTERS
SHORTENING
SUGAR
STIR
QUICK BREADS
GRAVIES
EGG WHITES
GENERAL

Speculaas Cookie Butter Dip

Speculaas are a type of Belgian spiced cookie—Lotus Biscoff cookies are the most popular brand in the USA—and they're basically edible hugs. When cookie butter went viral in the States a few years ago, I started making a creamy dip with the jar of cookie butter plus crumbled cookies mixed in for extra crunch and flavor. It's a fun shareable treat for a movie night or an easy dessert at the end of a meal.

- 1 (8-ounce) package cream cheese, at room temperature
- 1/4 cup powdered sugar
- 1/4 cup heavy cream
- 1 cup creamy cookie butter, such as Biscoff
- 1/2 teaspoon kosher salt
- Biscoff cookies, mini pretzels, and halved strawberries, for serving

1. In the bowl of a stand mixer fitted with the paddle attachment (or in a large bowl using a handheld mixer), combine the cream cheese, powdered sugar, and heavy cream. Beat on medium speed until the cream cheese is light and fluffy, about 2 minutes. Add the cookie butter and salt and beat again on low until combined. Increase the speed to medium and whip into an airy dip, about 1 minute more.
2. Transfer the dip to a serving bowl. Serve immediately or cover with plastic wrap and refrigerate for up to 3 days (bring to room temperature 30 minutes before serving).
3. Serve with cookies, pretzels, and strawberries alongside for dipping.

Grilled Melon and Prosciutto Salad

The first time I was in Florence, some friends and I wandered into a random local restaurant, ready for lunch. Unfortunately, the menu was all in Italian and the only word I recognized was "prosciutto," so I just pointed and ordered. I had never thought of pairing prosciutto and melon until then, but the sweet and salty was a fabulous combination. Grilling the melon cranks up the sweetness and crisps the prosciutto, making a perfect combo even better!

- 1 ripe cantaloupe (see Note)
- 1 ripe honeydew melon (see Note)
- Extra-virgin olive oil
- 6 ounces prosciutto

1. Cut the cantaloupe in half and use a spoon to scrape out and discard the seeds. Cut each half into four wedges. Lay each wedge on its side and run the knife between the melon and the peel to remove and discard the peel. Repeat these steps with the honeydew.
2. Lightly rub each wedge all over with olive oil, then wrap one piece of prosciutto around each wedge, pressing to adhere.
3. Prepare a grill or grill pan for high heat and lightly rub it with olive oil. Grill the wedges until the melon and prosciutto are nicely charred, about 3 minutes per side.
4. Arrange on a platter and drizzle with a little more olive oil before serving.

A ripe cantaloupe or honeydew should feel surprisingly heavy, have a sweet floral smell, and give slightly when you press around the stem area.

FLAT ANCHOVIES
WILD CAUGHT

Anchovy Spaghetti

This is probably the pasta dish I make most often at home. It's super easy to prepare, and I always have these ingredients lying around, so I can make it for lunch, dinner, or when company comes over without having to go to the grocery store. (This recipe serves two—or one, if you're like me—but can easily be multiplied to finish up the box of pasta or feed a crowd.) I think most people don't realize that when you cook anchovies, they just melt away into salty umami goodness and add so much flavor that isn't noticeably fishy. Don't underestimate them!

Kosher salt

½ pound dried spaghetti

¼ cup extra-virgin olive oil

6 anchovy fillets

3 garlic cloves, thinly sliced

Red pepper flakes

Juice of ½ lemon, for serving

Chopped fresh parsley, for serving

1. Bring a large pot of salted water to a boil over high heat. Add the pasta and cook until al dente according to the package directions, then drain.
2. In a large skillet, combine the olive oil, anchovies, garlic, and a pinch of red pepper flakes over medium heat. As the oil heats up, use a wooden spoon to stir and mash the anchovies until mostly dissolved. Let the garlic cook, stirring occasionally, until just beginning to brown on the edges, about 4 minutes. Add the drained pasta to the skillet and toss to thoroughly coat. Taste and adjust the seasoning, then remove from the heat.
3. Squeeze the lemon juice into the skillet and sprinkle plenty of chopped parsley over the top. Serve immediately, straight from the pan.

Warm Lemon Ricotta Dip

Italian food is pretty much universally loved around the world, and for good reason. There's an ease to Italian cooking that makes it accessible to everyone, plus a comforting balance of flavors that makes it very satisfying. This warm ricotta dip is the embodiment of that spirit. With its creamy, acidic, fatty, and just the right amount of spicy flavors, it's a simple but sophisticated affair.

- 1 (15-ounce) container full-fat ricotta cheese
- Zest and juice of 2 lemons
- 1 tablespoon finely chopped fresh rosemary
- 1 tablespoon extra-virgin olive oil, plus more for serving
- 1 teaspoon kosher salt
- Red pepper flakes, for serving
- Toasted Italian bread, for serving

1. Preheat the oven to 350°F.
2. In a small baking dish or an ovenproof skillet, stir together the ricotta, lemon zest and juice, rosemary, olive oil, and salt.
3. Bake for about 15 minutes, until the dip is warm and bubbling around the edges. Drizzle with a good amount of olive oil and finish with a pinch of red pepper flakes. Serve with slices of toasted bread alongside for dipping.

Roasted Flour Soup

I'll be you've never tried something like this in your life. Roasted flour soup is what I call a real hidden gem. I first had it backstage from the catering service during *Werq the World*—I had never tried anything like it! I was blown away by its rich, toasty flavor, but the soup is so simple to make. It's just butter, flour, beef broth, and red wine. But toasting the flour in the oven first gives such a rich depth of flavor, it makes it seem like there are hundreds of ingredients. This is perfect on a cold day!

- 1 cup all-purpose flour
- 4 tablespoons (½ stick) unsalted butter
- 4 cups beef broth
- ¼ cup dry red wine
- Kosher salt and freshly ground black pepper
- Shredded Gruyère cheese, for serving

1. Preheat the oven to 350°F.
2. On a baking sheet, spread out the flour evenly. Bake for 30 to 40 minutes, until the flour is dark golden brown and smells toasted.
3. In a Dutch oven, melt the butter over medium heat. Whisk in the flour to combine. Very slowly pour in the broth, whisking continuously to avoid lumps. Add the wine, a good pinch each of salt and pepper, and bring the soup to a boil. Reduce the heat to low and simmer, stirring occasionally, until thickened, 15 to 20 minutes. Taste and adjust the seasoning.
4. Divide the soup among bowls and top with Gruyère before serving.

Cheesy Bread Bowl Fondue

Switzerland is the home of great cheese, incredible chocolate, amazing cured meat, and, most famously, fondue. Growing up, I loved the anime *Heidi, Girl of the Alps*, and in the cartoon they were always eating gooey cheese. I wanted to reach through my TV and try it, so it was always my fantasy to one day eat gooey cheese in Switzerland. Years later, my dreams came true when I was booked for a gig in Switzerland, found a local wine bar, and had my long-awaited bread bowl of fondue. It did not disappoint and is still one of my favorite things to make for friends or even when I'm home alone. Healing my inner child, one dip at a time!

- 1 (6-inch) round bread loaf
- 4 tablespoons (1/2 stick) unsalted butter, melted
- 1 tablespoon finely chopped fresh parsley
- 4 ounces Gruyère cheese, grated
- 4 ounces Emmentaler or other Swiss cheese, grated
- 1/2 cup dry white wine
- 2 teaspoons cornstarch
- 1 teaspoon fresh lemon juice
- Freshly ground black pepper
- Freshly grated nutmeg, for garnish
- Accompaniments (boiled new potatoes, sliced apples or pears, and/or pickles), for serving

1. Preheat the oven to 350°F. Line a baking sheet with parchment paper.
2. Cut about 1 inch off the top of the loaf to expose the inside. Vertically cut and pull out the center bread, leaving about a 1-inch border of bread all around and taking care not to cut all the way through the bottom. Tear the center bread into roughly 1-inch pieces, and arrange on the prepared baking sheet. Toss the bread pieces with the butter and parsley. Bake for about 15 minutes, until the croutons are just slightly crisp on the edges.
3. Transfer the croutons to a serving platter along with any other accompaniments and set aside. Place the bread bowl on the same baking sheet.
4. In a small saucepan, combine both cheeses, the wine, cornstarch, and lemon juice. Cook over low heat, stirring often, until the cheeses are almost melted, about 5 minutes. Pour the mixture into the bread bowl and slide the baking sheet into the oven.
5. Bake for about 5 minutes, until the bread bowl is warm and the filling is smooth. Season with black pepper and garnish with a pinch of nutmeg, then serve immediately with the platter of croutons and accompaniments for dipping. Return the bowl to the oven for 5 to 10 minutes as needed to rewarm the fondue . . . if it lasts that long.

Pickled Herring Crudités Platter

Pickled herring has been a surprise love affair for me. When I was a kid in Michigan, a family friend invited us over for snacky appetizers of pickled herring, which made sense with the big Nordic population in the Midwest. Years later, I reconnected with this tangy, briny beauty in Sweden—because apparently, it was meant to be. This platter is a total snack upgrade: tangy herring, creamy sour cream, and crunchy pickled vegetables all on one very Scandinavian plate.

1 (32-ounce) jar pickled herring in wine sauce, drained

1 cup sour cream or crème fraîche

1 tablespoon finely chopped fresh dill

1 teaspoon finely chopped fresh chives

Kosher salt and freshly ground black pepper

Pumpernickel bread, for serving

Pickled Vegetables, for serving (recipe follows)

1. Chop the herring into small pieces or use a fork to mash it. In a medium bowl, mix the herring, sour cream, dill, chives, and a good pinch each of salt and pepper into a thick dip. Cover with plastic wrap and refrigerate until ready to serve, up to 24 hours.

2. Place the dip in the center of a serving platter. Arrange plenty of bread and pickled vegetables around the dip. To eat, spread some of the dip on the bread and arrange a few pickled vegetables on top.

Pickled Vegetables

Sliced vegetables, such as carrots, beets, celery, cucumbers, or radishes, in any combination

1 cup white wine vinegar

½ cup sugar

1 tablespoon kosher salt

1 teaspoon whole peppercorns

1 bay leaf

Pack two clean glass pint jars tightly with vegetables. In a small saucepan, combine the vinegar, sugar, salt, peppercorns, bay leaf, and 1 cup water. Bring to a boil over high heat, then spoon the hot brine into the jars, filling them to the brim. Screw on the lids tightly and let cool at room temperature for about 1 hour. Refrigerate for at least 24 hours and up to 2 weeks.

Open-Faced Shrimp Sandwiches

Sweden loves an open-faced sandwich, and so do I. At a lot of the cafés, and even at the airports, I kept seeing the same shrimp sandwich. I swear I even saw it at an Ikea! It's light and satisfying—basically a simple shrimp salad made with the cutest mini shrimp on (of course) rye bread. The lettuce layer keeps the bread from getting soggy, so don't skip it!

- 2 slices rye bread
- 4 butter lettuce leaves
- 2 hard-boiled large eggs, peeled and sliced
- ½ English cucumber, sliced
- 1 (6-ounce) can tiny shrimp, drained
- Juice of ½ lemon
- 1 tablespoon mayonnaise
- 1 teaspoon finely chopped fresh dill
- Kosher salt and freshly ground black pepper
- Lemon wedges, for serving

1. On each slice of bread, place 2 lettuce leaves. Shingle slices of egg and cucumber over the lettuce, dividing evenly between the bread.
2. In a small bowl, combine the shrimp, lemon juice, mayonnaise, dill, and a good pinch each of salt and pepper and gently toss just to coat. Pile the shrimp salad over the eggs and cucumbers.
3. Serve immediately with lemon wedges for squeezing and forks and knives for digging in.

ASIA

East Meets Feast

Even though I grew up in South Korea, I didn't really get to explore other Asian countries until later in life. As a broke Chicago-based queen serving looks in local bars, international travel wasn't exactly in the budget—but it was always on the vision board. After I mentioned on *Drag Race* that performing in Korea was my biggest dream, promoters reached out, and within weeks, I was on a plane. My first show there was sold out, with a line wrapped around the block. I spent the whole night holding back tears—talk about a homecoming!

While I was in Korea, promoters from Taiwan reached out, and off I went. I didn't know much about the country when I arrived, but I extended my trip almost immediately. The night markets were sublime, the food was life-changing, and now I refuse to stay for less than a week at a time because I never feel finished exploring.

Touring finally let me check off my list all the places I'd spent years double-tapping on Instagram—Japan, Singapore, Thailand, India. Hong Kong felt like stepping into a cyberpunk movie, so jam-packed and intricate. I reconnected with old friends there who took me on a winding street food tour I still think about all the time.

When I travel through Asia, I always feel right at home. There's this overwhelming sense of feeling welcome and embraced, like I'm right where I'm supposed to be. Plus, the hospitality is unmatched, and the food, of course, is fabulous.

Korean Hot Dogs

This popular Korean snack, known as *gamja-hotdog*, is sold by markets, food trucks, and street vendors everywhere. Think of it as the ultimate glow-up for an American corn dog: hot dog, cheese, battered, deep-fried, and somehow even better. (Ironically, it's become viral in the States as a "Korean corn dog.") I like mine with the extra flair of diced potatoes on the outside, which get a little bit crispy from the frying. But the real mic drop is the sprinkle of sugar added while they're still hot. Koreans love the flavor principle of *danjjan*—sweet-salty—and these hot dogs are its tastiest ambassador.

BATTER

- 2 tablespoons sugar
- 1 (¼ ounce) packet active dry yeast
- 2 teaspoons kosher salt
- 1½ cups all-purpose flour

HOT DOGS

- 1 (1-pound) large russet potato
- 4 hot dogs
- 4 slices mozzarella cheese, at room temperature
- 2 tablespoons all-purpose flour
- ½ cup panko breadcrumbs
- 2 quarts vegetable oil or other neutral oil, for frying

FOR SERVING

- Sugar
- Ketchup
- Yellow mustard

1 **Make the batter:** In a medium bowl, whisk together the sugar, yeast, and 1 cup warm water. Set aside until the yeast is foaming, about 5 minutes, then stir in the salt and flour until a sticky batter forms. Cover the bowl with plastic wrap and set aside to rise in a warm spot until doubled in size, about 1 hour.

2 **Meanwhile, make the hot dogs:** Peel the potato and cut it into ¼-inch pieces. In a medium bowl, soak the potatoes in cold water until ready to use.

3 Skewer the hot dogs onto wooden chopsticks. Wrap each hot dog with a slice of mozzarella (room-temperature cheese will wrap better) and set them on a plate, seam-side down. Chill in the freezer for 30 minutes so the cheese holds in place.

4 Drain the potatoes and pat dry with paper towels. On a large plate, toss the potatoes with the flour, then spread them out. On a separate large plate, spread out the panko.

5 In a Dutch oven or large saucepan, heat the oil over medium heat until it registers 350°F on an instant-read thermometer, or drop a few potatoes in the oil to test. They should start bubbling immediately.

Recipe continues

6 Working with one skewer at a time, swirl a hot dog in the batter to coat completely. Roll the battered skewer through the potatoes, lightly pressing to adhere. Then roll the skewer in the panko to coat completely.

7 Using tongs, lower the skewer in the oil and cook for about 5 minutes, flipping halfway through, until golden brown all over. Transfer to paper towels to drain and sprinkle with sugar. Repeat with the remaining skewers, allowing the oil to return to temperature between batches.

8 Arrange the warm hot dogs on a platter. Finish with a drizzle of ketchup and mustard before serving.

Birthday Seaweed Soup

In Korea, and in Korean American households, when you wake up on your birthday, your mom will have a giant pot of this soup waiting for you. After a Korean woman gives birth, she eats this soup every day for a month because the nutritional benefits help her body heal. So on your birthday, it's a little nod to your mom, a "thanks for bringing me into this world" moment. But honestly, it's so delicious we eat it year-round, birthday or not. So much Korean food has been commercialized in the USA, but this one still feels like a secret. Shhh, keep it between us!

- ½ ounce miyeok or other edible dried seaweed
- 1 tablespoon vegetable oil or other neutral oil
- 1 pound beef brisket or skirt steak, thinly sliced
- 5 garlic cloves, minced
- 2 tablespoons soy sauce
- Toasted sesame oil, for serving

1. In a medium bowl, submerge the seaweed in cold water and set aside to soak for 30 minutes. Drain.
2. In a Dutch oven, heat the vegetable oil over high heat until it shimmers. Add the beef and cook, stirring often, until lightly browned, about 2 minutes. Stir in the garlic and cook until fragrant, about 30 seconds, then add 8 cups water along with the soy sauce and drained seaweed.
3. Cover and cook for about 10 minutes, then reduce the heat to low and simmer for 40 minutes, until the beef is tender and the broth is flavorful. While the soup simmers, periodically lift the lid and use a spoon to skim and discard any foam from the surface.
4. Divide the soup between two bowls and finish with a drizzle of sesame oil before serving.

Budae Jjigae

This dish was born during the Korean War, when South Korean soldiers were introduced to American military rations for the first time. Shelf-stable ingredients like Spam, kielbasa, baked beans, and American cheese were simmered in a classic soup base of gochujang and kimchi. What started as the meeting of Korean and American culture is now, still, served in restaurants and fully accepted as part of traditional Korean cuisine. If you have a portable burner, it's a great dish to serve in the middle of the table as a very social and interactive dinner entrée.

- 6 garlic cloves, minced
- 2 tablespoons gochujang
- 1 tablespoon gochugaru or red pepper flakes (optional)
- 1 tablespoon soy sauce
- 1 teaspoon sugar
- ¼ head green cabbage, quartered, cored, and thinly sliced
- ½ white onion, thinly sliced
- 8 button mushrooms, thinly sliced
- 4 scallions, cut into 1-inch pieces
- ½ cup chopped kimchi
- 4 ounces firm tofu, drained and thinly sliced
- 4 ounces Spam, thinly sliced
- 4 ounces kielbasa, sliced into rounds
- ¼ cup baked beans
- 1 (3-ounce) package instant ramen noodles, flavor packet discarded
- 1 slice American cheese
- 4 cups beef broth

1. In a small bowl, stir together the garlic, gochujang, gochugaru (if using), soy sauce, and sugar.

2. In a large sauté pan or saucepan, layer the cabbage, onions, mushrooms, and scallions along the bottom. Spoon the gochujang mixture into the center. Arrange piles of kimchi, tofu, Spam, kielbasa, and baked beans around the perimeter. Place the uncooked ramen in the center and set the slice of American cheese on top. Pour in 2 to 3 cups of the broth until it just touches the ingredients around the edge.

3. To serve in true Korean fashion, set a portable burner in the center of the table and let the stew come to a simmer over medium heat (see Note). Once the liquid is bubbling, lightly mix the ingredients to submerge them. When the ramen is tender, let everyone dive in, using a ladle to spoon the broth into small bowls and chopsticks or tongs to fish out the ingredients. Add more broth as needed as the stew boils down.

NOTE If you don't have a portable burner, set the stew over medium heat. When it's bubbling, mixed, and the ramen is tender, bring to the table to serve. Warm up over the stove and add more broth as needed.

Creamy Kimchi Noodles

Korean ingredients, especially kimchi, have become increasingly popular in the United States and have created an interesting culinary dialogue between the two countries. This pasta is a fully Americanized dish using Korean staples. (Conversely, Korean Hot Dogs, page 145, is a perfect example of Koreans interpreting American food.) Think of it as a spicy, garlicky riff on pasta with vodka sauce—with diced kimchi supplying just the right hit of tang to cut through the richness. It's fusion in the best way—kimchi crashing the creamy pasta party and taking it to the next level.

- 1 pound dried spaghetti
- 4 slices bacon, diced
- 1 medium white onion, diced
- 4 garlic cloves, minced
- 1 cup chopped kimchi, plus 3 tablespoons kimchi brine
- ¼ cup soy sauce
- ½ cup heavy cream

FOR SERVING

- Thinly sliced scallions
- Toasted sesame seeds
- 4 fried eggs (optional)

1. Bring a large pot of water to a boil over high heat. Add the spaghetti and cook until al dente according to the package directions, then drain.
2. Meanwhile, in a large skillet, cook the bacon over medium heat until the fat has rendered and the bacon is crisp, 6 to 8 minutes. Add the onions and garlic and cook, stirring often, until the onions are soft, about 5 minutes. Stir in the kimchi, brine, soy sauce, and heavy cream. Bring to a simmer, stirring continuously, until the sauce is thick and uniform, about 2 minutes. Add the spaghetti and use tongs to toss and coat.
3. Divide the noodles among four bowls. Finish with a sprinkle of scallions and toasted sesame seeds. Optional, but highly recommended, is placing a fried egg sunny-side-up on top of each bowl. Serve immediately.

TERRA

Bossam

Bossam is the taste of childhood for every Korean kid. My mom made this all the time because it's such an easy family dinner, and now I love making it for my friends in LA because it's a big hands-on spread that lends itself to good dinner conversation. Pork belly is cheap and really hard to mess up—it gets more tender the longer you cook it. And there are endless ways to serve bossam, with any mix of banchan, which are small side dishes meant to be shared: kimchi, steamed and pickled vegetables, or stir-fried anchovies. My only requirement is a small bowl of ssamjang, a thick, spicy paste made from fermented soybeans (doenjang), which makes every bite incredibly flavorful.

PORK

- 2 pounds pork belly
- 1 large white onion, quartered
- 4 scallions, cut into 2-inch pieces
- 1 (2-inch) piece fresh ginger, peeled and smashed
- 8 garlic cloves, smashed
- 2 tablespoons doenjang
- 1 tablespoon dark brown sugar
- 1 tablespoon instant coffee granules

SSAMJANG

- ¼ cup doenjang
- 1 tablespoon gochujang
- 2 scallions, thinly sliced
- 1 garlic clove, minced
- 2 teaspoons toasted sesame seeds
- 2 teaspoons dark brown sugar
- 2 teaspoons toasted sesame oil

1 **Make the pork:** Rinse the pork belly thoroughly under cold water and pat dry with paper towels. In a large Dutch oven, combine the pork, onions, scallions, ginger, garlic, doenjang, brown sugar, coffee granules, and 8 cups cold water.

2 Cover the pot with the lid slightly ajar and cook over high heat for 1 hour. Uncover and use tongs to flip the pork. Reduce the heat to medium, cover in the same fashion, and cook for another 30 minutes. Then reduce the heat to low and simmer for 30 minutes. Transfer the pork to a plate and let cool to room temperature, about 1 hour. The pork can be served when cooled or transferred to an airtight container and stored in the refrigerator for up to 3 days (bring to room temperature before serving).

3 **Meanwhile, make the ssamjang:** In a small bowl, stir together the doenjang, gochujang, scallions, garlic, sesame seeds, brown sugar, and sesame oil. Use immediately or cover with plastic wrap and refrigerate for up to 3 days (bring to room temperature before serving).

Recipe and ingredients continue

4 To serve, thinly slice the pork and arrange on a platter, along with the lettuce leaves, sliced garlic and jalapeños, the bowl of ssamjang, and any banchan, if using.

NOTE To eat bossam like a pro, hold a lettuce leaf in your hand. Place a piece of pork in the center, then add a dab of ssamjang, a piece or two of garlic and jalapeño, and a small amount of any banchan. Fold the lettuce up like a package and pop it in your mouth.

FOR SERVING

Butter lettuce leaves

Thinly sliced garlic

Thinly sliced jalapeños

Banchan of your choice (optional)

TERRA

오뚜기
OTTOGI
SESAME
OIL
옛날 참기름
PURE SESAME

Bibim-Guksu

My mom would make this dish for us a lot growing up, especially during hot summer days in Korea. And when I say quick and easy, I mean quick and easy! The noodles only take three minutes to boil, then they're rinsed and served in a chilled bowl so they're extra cold and refreshing. It's like a cool breeze in a bowl. My mom grew her own lettuce in our backyard that she would chop up and add, so if you have fresh greens around, go ahead and use them. Like the Anchovy Spaghetti (page 131), this is another dish where I always have all the ingredients handy and can make it whenever I'm craving it. Eating this always reminds me of the summer days of my childhood in Korea.

- 2 large eggs
- 8 ounces somyeon noodles or any thin rice noodles
- ½ pound kimchi, finely chopped, plus ¼ cup kimchi brine
- 2 garlic cloves, minced
- 3 tablespoons gochujang
- 1 tablespoon gochugaru or red pepper flakes (optional)
- 2 teaspoons soy sauce
- 2 teaspoons sugar
- ½ English cucumber, cut into matchsticks
- Toasted sesame oil, for serving
- Toasted sesame seeds, for serving

1. Prepare a bowl of ice water. Bring a large saucepan of water to a boil over high heat. Use a spoon to gently lower the eggs into the water. Boil for 7 minutes for a jammy yolk or up to 10 minutes for a set yolk. Use the spoon to lift out the eggs and transfer to the ice water to stop cooking.
2. In the same saucepan of boiling water, stir in the noodles. Boil for about 3 minutes, stirring often, until tender. Drain and rinse under cold water to cool completely. Shake to drain well.
3. In a large bowl, combine the kimchi, brine, garlic, gochujang, gochugaru (if using), soy sauce, and sugar. Add the noodles and toss to coat.
4. Transfer the dressed noodles to a serving bowl and pile the cucumbers on top. Peel the eggs, cut in half, and set on top, yolk-side up. Finish with a drizzle of sesame oil and a sprinkle of sesame seeds before serving.

Breakfast Scallion Pancakes

The first time I went to Taiwan I had no idea what to expect—it was just another booking for me. But Taiwanese night-market culture changed my life. Everything was very good and very cheap, but the scallion pancakes were the biggest standout to me. They're crispy, flaky, oniony, and fried, a perfect canvas for a mix of toppings—almost like a breakfast burrito, but better. This version is my dream breakfast sandwich, with egg, ham, and gooey cheese glued to the pancake. And because the prepared dough can be stored in the refrigerator and fried to order, I can make my dreams come true all week!

SCALLION PANCAKE DOUGH

- 4½ cups all-purpose flour, plus more for rolling
- 1 teaspoon kosher salt
- 2 cups boiling water
- 8 scallions, thinly sliced
- ½ teaspoon white pepper
- 1 cup vegetable oil or other neutral oil

TOPPING

- 4 tablespoons vegetable oil or other neutral oil
- 8 large eggs
- 8 slices deli ham
- 8 slices American cheese

1 **Make the scallion pancake dough:** In a large bowl, stir together 4 cups of the flour and the salt. Slowly pour in the boiling water while stirring continuously. When the dough is cool enough to handle, knead it in the bowl until well combined, about 2 minutes. Cover the bowl with plastic wrap and refrigerate for at least 1 hour or overnight.

2 Remove the dough from the refrigerator and let it rest at room temperature for 15 minutes for easy rolling.

3 Meanwhile, in a small heat-resistant bowl, stir together the remaining ½ cup flour, scallions, and white pepper. In a small skillet, heat the vegetable oil over high heat until it shimmers. Carefully pour the oil into the bowl with the flour-scallion mixture—it'll bubble at first—and stir to make a smooth paste.

4 Lightly dust a work surface with flour. Divide the dough into four equal portions and keep them covered with a clean kitchen towel. Working one portion at a time, roll into a rough rectangle about ⅛ inch thick, using more flour as needed to prevent sticking. Brush about 2 tablespoons of the scallion paste evenly over the surface of the dough. Fold the dough in thirds like a letter, then fold it in half across

Recipe continues

the width. Roll again to make a long rectangle, about ½ inch thick. Starting at one short end, tightly roll along the dough to make a large coil and pinch to seal the seam. Repeat with the remaining dough pieces and paste. The dough can be used immediately or wrapped in plastic and stored in the refrigerator for up to 3 days.

5 Working with one coil at a time, set the dough so the seam is facing up. Roll into a roughly 8-inch round. (Check the diameter of your skillet to be sure the scallion pancake is the same size or a little smaller.)

6 **Make the topping:** In a medium nonstick skillet, heat 1 tablespoon of the vegetable oil over medium heat. Beat 2 of the eggs in a small bowl. When the oil is just beginning to smoke, lay the scallion pancake in the skillet. Cook until lightly charred on the bottom, about 2 minutes. Flip and cook until lightly charred on the other side, about 2 minutes more. Remove the pancake to a plate and immediately pour the beaten eggs into the skillet. Tilt the skillet to spread the eggs along the bottom, then scatter in 2 slices each of the ham and cheese, then the scallion pancake. Cook until the eggs are just set, about 90 seconds, then turn out the pancake back onto the same plate. Cut into quarters and serve immediately.

7 Wipe out the skillet and repeat the process with the remaining scallion pancake dough, oil, eggs, ham, and cheese, making one pancake at a time.

Bubble Waffles

Bubble waffles, or egg waffles, are basically the A-list celebrities of Taiwanese sweets. Their puffy texture is their signature, made in special waffle irons—easy to order online—to create little bubbles on the surface, and they're served plain or with fruit, spreads, or ice cream. The waffles themselves usually come in different flavors, too. This recipe is for the base batter, but you can add matcha or chocolate if you're feeling fancy (see Note). Sure, you can use a regular waffle iron, but why deny yourself the joy of crunching those crispy, air-filled bubbles?

- 1¼ cups all-purpose flour
- ¼ cup tapioca starch or cornstarch
- 2 teaspoons baking powder
- ½ teaspoon kosher salt
- 2 large eggs
- ¾ cup sugar
- 2 tablespoons vegetable oil or other neutral oil, plus more for greasing
- 1 teaspoon pure vanilla extract

1. In a medium bowl, whisk together the flour, tapioca starch, baking powder, and salt.
2. Fill a small saucepan with about 1 inch of water and set a heat-resistant medium bowl on top, making sure the bowl doesn't touch the water. Whisk together the eggs and sugar in the bowl. Set the saucepan and bowl over medium heat. As the water comes to a simmer, continuously whisk until the eggs thicken slightly, 5 to 7 minutes. Return the bowl to the work surface.
3. Whisk the vegetable oil, vanilla, and ¾ cup water into the egg mixture. Fold in the dry ingredients until combined. Cover the bowl with plastic wrap and refrigerate the batter for at least 1 hour or overnight.
4. Preheat the waffle iron according to the manufacturer's directions and lightly grease both sides with vegetable oil. When the machine is ready, pour in about 1 cup of batter and close. When the waffle is cooked, transfer it to a plate and use the batter to make two more. Serve warm.

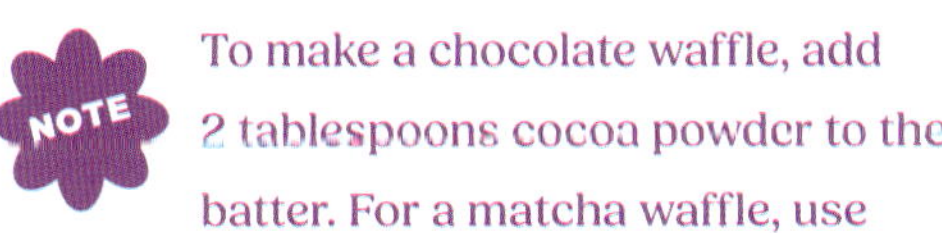

NOTE To make a chocolate waffle, add 2 tablespoons cocoa powder to the batter. For a matcha waffle, use 1 tablespoon matcha powder.

Pineapple Cake Bars

In Taiwan, pineapple cakes are everywhere, individually wrapped and ready to brighten your day. Whenever I go, I usually stock up on them to bring back for friends—but who am I kidding? A lot of them are for me. For years, I've wanted to make my own version, but nobody has time to sit there and individually craft small cakes. So I decided to break the rules a bit and make a whole pan that can be sliced like brownies for an easy batch of my favorite little treats.

FILLING

- 1 (20-ounce) can crushed pineapple, drained
- ½ cup granulated sugar
- 2 tablespoons corn syrup
- 1 tablespoon cornstarch
- 1 teaspoon fresh lemon juice
- ½ teaspoon kosher salt

DOUGH

- Nonstick cooking spray
- 2 cups all-purpose flour
- ¼ cup powdered sugar
- 2 tablespoons cornstarch
- 1 teaspoon kosher salt
- 1 cup (2 sticks) unsalted butter, cut into small cubes and chilled
- 2 large egg yolks

1. **Make the filling:** In a medium saucepan, spread the pineapple in an even layer. Cook over medium heat, stirring often, until the pineapple is almost dry, about 10 minutes. Stir in the granulated sugar, corn syrup, cornstarch, lemon juice, and salt. Cook, stirring often, until the mixture is golden and jammy, about 10 minutes more. Transfer to a bowl and let cool for 30 minutes. Cover with plastic wrap and chill in the refrigerator for at least 2 hours and up to 2 days.

2. **Make the dough:** Preheat the oven to 350°F. Line an 8-inch-square baking dish with parchment paper, leaving a 1-inch overhang on all sides. Coat the parchment with nonstick spray.

3. In a food processor, combine the flour, powdered sugar, cornstarch, and salt. Pulse 2 times, then add the butter and pulse 6 times to form a clumpy dough. Add the egg yolks and process until the dough pulls together, about 30 seconds. (You can also mix this in a large bowl by pinching in the butter and stirring in the yolks with a wooden spoon.)

4. Press half of the dough along the bottom of the prepared baking dish, then smooth the pineapple filling evenly over the top. Crumble the remaining dough over the filling, covering it completely.

5. Bake for 15 to 20 minutes, rotating the pan halfway through, until the top is golden brown. Remove and let cool completely in the pan, about 1 hour. Use the parchment overhang to transfer to a cutting board and slice into 12 bars. Serve immediately or store in an airtight container at room temperature for up to 3 days.

Ice Cream Wraps

One of the best desserts I've ever had was in Jiufen, a dreamy mountain town in Taiwan that looks straight out of *Spirited Away*. I saw so many food vendors in the street selling this ice cream wrap, and I couldn't imagine what the flavors would be like together. On paper it's a little confusing—a crepe base, taro ice cream, grated candied peanuts, and cilantro—but somehow it all works together. I never expected cilantro to be that good (or good at all) in a dessert, but it was! Whenever I can get my hands on taro ice cream, I know exactly what to do with it.

- ¾ cup all-purpose flour
- 2 tablespoons tapioca starch or cornstarch
- ½ teaspoon kosher salt
- 1 teaspoon vegetable oil or other neutral oil, plus more as needed
- Taro ice cream or vanilla ice cream
- Peanut brittle candy
- Fresh cilantro leaves

1. In a medium bowl, whisk together the flour, tapioca starch, salt, and 1¼ cups warm water to create the crepe batter.

2. Heat a medium nonstick skillet over low heat for 5 minutes. Pour in the vegetable oil and use a paper towel to wipe it around the skillet. Pour about ½ cup of batter into the skillet and swirl to coat. Cook until the bottom is set and lightly browned, about 4 minutes. Flip and cook until lightly browned on the other side, about 2 minutes more. Transfer to a plate. Repeat with the remaining batter to make four total wraps, wiping more oil on the skillet if necessary.

3. On each of four plates, lay out one wrap. Place two scoops of ice cream in the center of each. Use a box grater to grate a generous amount of peanut brittle over the tops, then finish with cilantro leaves.

4. Tuck in the sides of the wrap, then roll up like a burrito and serve immediately.

Okonomiyaki

Imagine if an omelet and a pancake had a baby—that's okonomiyaki. It's a thick batter made from eggs, flour, and shredded cabbage, with a variety of fillings and toppings. My first time in Japan, a friend took me to a restaurant where they made it right at the table and served it steaming hot. This at-home version sticks to the basics, which you can customize with meats, vegetables, and fillings as you get the hang of it. Depending on what you put in it, okonomiyaki can actually be a relatively healthy, filling meal!

SAUCE

- 1/4 cup ketchup
- 2 tablespoons Worcestershire sauce
- 2 tablespoons oyster sauce or 1 tablespoon soy sauce
- 1 tablespoon sugar

OKONOMIYAKI

- 1 1/4 cups all-purpose flour
- 1/2 teaspoon kosher salt
- 1/2 teaspoon baking powder
- 3 large eggs
- 1/2 head green cabbage, cored and thinly sliced (about 4 cups)
- 1 large carrot, grated
- 2 scallions, thinly sliced, whites and greens separated
- 2 tablespoons vegetable oil or other neutral oil

- Kewpie mayonnaise (see Note), for serving
- Bonito flakes, for serving

1 **Make the sauce:** In a small bowl, whisk together the ketchup, Worcestershire sauce, oyster sauce, and sugar. Transfer to a small squeeze bottle (or to a zip-top bag; snip a small corner off the bag before squeezing) and refrigerate until ready to use, up to 3 days.

2 **Make the okonomiyaki:** In a large bowl, whisk together the flour, salt, and baking powder. Whisk in the eggs, then gradually pour in 1 cup water while still whisking until a thick batter forms. Add the cabbage, carrots, and scallion whites and toss to coat well, then set aside the batter to rest for 10 minutes.

3 In a large nonstick skillet, heat the vegetable oil over medium heat until it shimmers. Scrape in the batter and smooth it into an even layer. Cover and cook for about 8 minutes, until the bottom is golden brown and crisp. Run a spatula around and underneath and shake the skillet to make sure the okonomiyaki is loose. Flip and cook, uncovered, until the other side is golden brown, about 6 minutes. Run the spatula underneath and shake the skillet again, then slide the okonomiyaki onto a serving plate.

4 Squeeze strips of the sauce and mayo on top. Sprinkle on the scallion greens, then finish with bonito flakes before serving.

NOTE Kewpie mayonnaise is a Japanese mayonnaise with a tangy and umami-rich flavor. It's usually available in the mayo aisle but can also be purchased at an Asian grocery store or online.

Pasta Napolitan

Japanese people have a fascination with Italian food to the point where they have created their own Italian-Japanese fusion called *itameshi*. There's even a chain restaurant, Saizeriya, that specializes in itameshi. One of their most famous dishes is Napolitan, a pasta dish named after Naples that would make any actual Neapolitan pass out from shock. It's a mix of spaghetti, onions, peppers, sausage, and—wait for it—ketchup. I know! It might seem really odd, but it actually tastes incredible! Plus, it's always interesting to see how food travels and evolves (and fuses) around the world.

- Kosher salt
- 1 pound dried spaghetti
- 2 tablespoons extra-virgin olive oil
- 8 ounces Japanese sausage, such as kurobuta or arabiki, or any smoked sausage, thinly sliced on on angle
- 1 white onion, halved and thinly sliced
- 1 green bell pepper, thinly sliced
- 2 garlic cloves, minced
- ½ cup ketchup
- 1 tablespoon Worcestershire sauce
- 1 teaspoon sugar
- Freshly grated Parmesan cheese, for serving

1. Bring a large pot of salted water to a boil over high heat. Add the pasta and cook until al dente according to the package directions. Reserve 1 cup of the pasta cooking water, then drain.

2. Meanwhile, in a large sauté pan or skillet, heat the olive oil over medium heat until it shimmers. Add the sausage, onions, peppers, and garlic. Cook, stirring often, until the vegetables are tender and the sausage is warmed through, about 3 minutes. Stir in the ketchup, Worcestershire sauce, and sugar. Remove from the heat until the pasta is ready.

3. Add the spaghetti and about ¼ cup of the pasta cooking water to the sauce in the pan and return to medium heat. Use tongs to toss the pasta to coat completely, adding another splash of pasta cooking water as needed to help the sauce move easily. Simmer until the sauce is glossy and thick, 1 to 2 minutes more.

4. Divide the pasta among four plates and top with plenty of Parmesan before serving.

生
貯蔵酒
DRAFT SAKE
白鶴
JUNMAI
300ml

Oyakodon
(THE CHICKEN AND THE EGG)

When I lived in Chicago, there was a Japanese diner around the corner from my apartment. Calling it a diner is generous, actually. It looked more like someone's living room, with Japanese dramas playing on the television and random bobbleheads everywhere. The very sweet Japanese family who ran it kept really odd hours, sometimes open late, sometimes only for a few hours in the middle of the day. But it all added to the fun and mystery, like wandering into a friend's house. After working my way through most of the menu, I found my favorite order, which included oyakodon. It's a cheap, filling, and delicious mix of ingredients: chicken thighs, scrambled eggs, and scallions served over rice. I also like to add a pinch of togarashi, a Japanese spice pepper blend, for an extra kick. When I left Chicago, I took this recipe with me and it's still one of my favorite things to make.

½ pound boneless, skinless chicken thighs, cut into 1-inch pieces

1 tablespoon sake or cooking wine

4 large eggs

½ white onion, thinly sliced

½ cup dashi or chicken broth

2 tablespoons soy sauce

2 tablespoons mirin

2 teaspoons sugar

FOR SERVING

Cooked white rice (see page 175)

Thinly sliced scallions

Togarashi spice blend

1. In a medium bowl, toss together the chicken and sake. Set aside to marinate for about 5 minutes. In a small bowl, lightly beat the eggs until the yolks are broken but the whites are still mostly separated.
2. In a medium nonstick skillet, arrange the onion slices in an even layer. Pour the dashi, soy sauce, mirin, and sugar over the top. Cook over medium heat, stirring occasionally, until the sauce begins to simmer, about 3 minutes. Add the chicken in an even layer and cook, stirring occasionally, until it is cooked through, about 6 minutes.
3. Slowly pour in the eggs in a spiral, starting in the center and working out to the edge of the skillet. Reduce the heat to low, cover, and cook until the eggs are almost set, 4 to 6 minutes. Remove from the heat.
4. Fill two bowls with about 1 cup of cooked rice each, then spoon the oyakodon on top, dividing evenly. Finish each with a sprinkle of scallions and a pinch of togarashi before serving.

Roast Beef Bowls

After walking around in Shinjuku all day, I saw a line of people waiting outside a roast beef spot. The restaurant looked . . . humble, to put it nicely, but I was too hungry to keep walking, so I got in line with everyone else. Imagining an American-style deli type of sliced roast beef, I thought, How good could this possibly be? Answer: Very. These were slices of fresh, tender, melt-in-your-mouth roast beef, layered on a mound of rice, with an egg yolk on top and horseradish cream on the side. I understood the wait! It was perfect, and I couldn't wait to re-create it myself!

ROAST BEEF

- 2 pounds rump roast, bottom round, or sirloin tip
- Kosher salt and freshly ground black pepper
- 1 tablespoon vegetable oil or other neutral oil

FOR SERVING

- Cooked white rice (recipe opposite)
- 4 large egg yolks
- Cream-style horseradish
- Thinly sliced scallions

1 **Make the roast beef:** Bring the roast to room temperature about 1 hour before cooking.

2 Place a rack in the center of the oven and another just below it. Preheat the oven to 375°F. Line a baking sheet with aluminum foil and place it on the lower rack.

3 Pat the roast dry with paper towels and season generously all over with salt and pepper. Place the roast directly on the center rack so the baking sheet below can catch the drippings. Roast for about 30 minutes, until the outside is browned, then reduce the temperature to 225°F. Continue roasting for about 1½ hours, until an instant-read thermometer registers 135 to 140°F when inserted into the center of the meat and it is nicely pink inside.

4 Place the finished roast on a cutting board and tent with foil. Let rest for 20 minutes before thinly slicing with a very sharp knife.

5 To assemble, fill four bowls with about 1 cup of cooked rice each, mounding it in the center. Lay overlapping slices of roast beef over the rice, then nestle an egg yolk in the center. (If you're worried about eating a raw egg, just use a fried one instead.) Spoon some horseradish on the side and finish with a sprinkle of scallions before serving.

White Rice

MAKES 4 CUPS

1½ cups short-grain white rice

Kosher salt

In a small bowl, rinse the rice under cold water several times, swishing it to release the starch, until the water runs clear. In a medium saucepan, combine the rice with 1⅔ cups warm water and a pinch of salt. Cover the pan and let the rice soak for 30 minutes. Set over high heat, bring to a boil, then reduce the heat to low. Simmer until the water has been absorbed, about 12 minutes. Remove from the heat and let the rice rest, still covered, for 10 minutes. Fluff with a fork or rice paddle. Store any leftover rice in an airtight container in the refrigerator for up to 5 days.

Kaya Toast

Kaya is a sweet coconut jam, easy to find online or in some Asian groceries, and it's often sandwiched on toasted bread with a thick slab of cold butter. On the side is a bowl with a runny egg and a splash of soy sauce. You take the sweet sandwich, dip it in the rich and salty egg, and somehow it all works together. They serve this toast everywhere in Singapore, and I saw so many locals eating it when I was there. Finally one day I decided to order it for myself. You just have to trust me: Your breakfast game is about to level up!

- 2 slices white sandwich bread, crusts discarded
- Kaya jam
- ½ stick salted or unsalted butter, very cold, thinly sliced
- 1 poached egg (see Note)
- Soy sauce, for serving
- White pepper, for serving

1. Toast the slices of bread. Spread a generous amount of kaya jam on one side of each slice. Arrange the butter on top of the jam on one of the slices. Press the other slice on top to make a sandwich.
2. Place the poached egg in a small bowl. Top with a drizzle of soy sauce and a pinch of white pepper.
3. Serve the sandwich immediately, with the bowl of poached egg alongside.

NOTE To poach an egg in its shell as they do in the Singapore cafés, submerge the egg in warm water for 10 minutes to bring to room temperature. In a small saucepan, bring 4 cups water to a rolling boil over high heat. Remove the pan from the heat and stir in 1 cup cold water. Use a spoon to gently lower in the egg, cover, and let sit for 15 minutes. Crack the egg into a bowl, and a perfectly poached beauty will slip out. This method can be performed with up to 4 eggs at a time.

AYAM
SPICE PASTE
CURRY NOODLE
MEDIUM

Laksa Noodle Soup

On my first night in Singapore, I wandered through a night market and bought this rich and delicious soup from a stall. It was like a more nuanced and textured answer to a brothy bowl of ramen or pho. This is one of the signature dishes of Singapore, loaded with rice noodles, vegetables, and your choice of proteins—my favorite is pillowy deep-fried squares of tofu puffs, which are sold vacuumed-packed but swell like a sponge in the soup. The soup gets its complexity from laksa paste, a flavorful condiment made of shrimp paste, dried chiles, spices, and aromatics. Laksa paste and tofu puffs can be purchased online or in some Asian grocery stores.

SERVES 4

2 tablespoons vegetable oil or other neutral oil

1 lemongrass stalk, outer layer removed, minced

4 garlic cloves, minced

1 (4-inch) piece fresh ginger, peeled and grated

¾ cup laksa paste

2 cups chicken broth or vegetable broth

1 (13.5-ounce) can full-fat coconut milk

1 tablespoon fish sauce or soy sauce, plus more as needed

8 ounces rice vermicelli noodles

1 (4- to 6-ounce) package tofu puffs

FOR SERVING

Bean sprouts

Crispy fried shallots

Sliced fresh red chiles

Chopped fresh cilantro

Lime wedges

1. In a Dutch oven, heat the vegetable oil over medium heat until it shimmers. Add the lemongrass, garlic, and ginger and stir until fragrant, about 10 seconds. Add the laksa paste and cook, stirring often, until simmering, about 1 minute.
2. Pour in the chicken broth, coconut milk, and fish sauce. Cover and simmer until the flavors are married, about 10 minutes. Taste and adjust the seasoning, adding a splash more fish sauce if it needs salt.
3. Meanwhile, soak the vermicelli according to the package directions, then drain. Add to the soup and simmer until cooked through, about 2 minutes. Remove the soup from the heat and stir in the tofu puffs.
4. Divide the soup among four bowls and top each bowl with bean sprouts, fried shallots, chiles, cilantro, and a lime wedge before serving.

Chilli Shrimp

Before I go to a country, I love to research the food. When I was doing my research for Singapore, I kept coming across chilli crab. As soon as we got there, my friend and I beelined to a chilli crab restaurant. It was very good, with layers of seasoning, salty taucu paste made from fermented soybeans, and a sweet chile sauce. But it was very expensive! So when I wanted to create these flavors and textures at home without breaking the bank, using shrimp in place of the crab seemed like the obvious choice. I love using whole shrimp—heads, shells, tails, and all. It gives you that satisfying messy, hands-on experience of cracking them open to reach the tender, sweet meat. A little cheaper, a lot easier, and every bit as addictive.

1 large shallot, coarsely chopped
4 fresh red chiles, stemmed and coarsely chopped
4 garlic cloves, coarsely chopped
1 (2-inch) piece fresh ginger, peeled and coarsely chopped
2 tablespoons taucu paste or miso paste
¼ cup vegetable oil or other neutral oil
1 (10.75-ounce) can tomato puree
¾ cup sweet chile sauce, such as Mae Ploy
2 tablespoons unseasoned rice vinegar
2 pounds shell-on jumbo shrimp (see Note)
Chopped fresh cilantro, for serving
Thinly sliced scallions, for serving

1. In a blender, combine the shallots, chiles, garlic, ginger, taucu paste, and 2 tablespoons cold water. Blend on medium speed until a thick chile paste forms, about 1 minute, adding a splash more water as needed to help everything come together.

2. In a large saucepan, heat the vegetable oil over medium heat until it shimmers. Add the chile paste from the blender and cook, stirring continuously, until thickened, about 3 minutes. Add the tomato puree and cook, stirring occasionally, until reduced by half, about 8 minutes.

3. Add the chile sauce, vinegar, and 2 cups water. Increase the heat to high and bring to a boil. Remove from the heat, add the shrimp, and stir to coat. Cover and let sit for about 5 minutes, until the shrimp are curled up and their shells are bright red.

4. Pour the shrimp and sauce into a large serving bowl. Let cool for 10 minutes, then garnish with cilantro and scallions. Set in the center of the table and let everyone peel and eat.

NOTE If your shrimp have long whiskers, use kitchen shears to trim them off before adding to the sauce.

Yum Woon Sen

I didn't have a ton of exposure to Thai food until I moved to Chicago, where Thai restaurants are everywhere, much like Chinese places are in other cities. When I first tried yum woon sen, it immediately shoved pad thai and pad see ew to the side and became my go-to order. It's a spicy, tangy noodle salad with a playground of textures: fresh veggies, chewy noodles, snappy shrimp, and crunchy peanuts. It's the kind of dish that has you saying "Just one more bite," until you realize the whole bowl's gone.

- 1 (3.75-ounce) package bean threads or glass noodles
- 3 garlic cloves, grated
- 2 or 3 fresh Thai chiles, stemmed and minced
- 2 tablespoons palm sugar or light brown sugar
- Juice of 2 limes
- ¼ cup plus 1 tablespoon fish sauce
- 1 large tomato, diced
- ½ white onion, thinly sliced
- 2 celery stalks, thinly sliced
- 1 pound jumbo shrimp, peeled (tails left on) and deveined
- 1 pound ground chicken or pork
- Chopped roasted peanuts and chopped fresh cilantro, for serving

1. Bring a large saucepan of water to a boil over high heat. In a medium bowl, cover the noodles with warm water and set aside to soak for 10 minutes until soft.
2. Meanwhile, in a large bowl, whisk together the garlic, chiles, palm sugar, lime juice, and ¼ cup of the fish sauce. Add the tomatoes, onions, and celery and toss to coat.
3. When the saucepan of water is boiling, add the shrimp and cook until bright pink and opaque, about 1 minute. Use a slotted spoon to transfer the shrimp to the bowl of dressing and toss to coat. Leave the water boiling over high heat.
4. Drain the noodles and use kitchen scissors to cut them into shorter segments. Add to the boiling water and cook until cooked through, about 2 minutes. Drain and rinse under cold water to stop the cooking. Shake to drain completely, then add to the bowl with the shrimp and toss to coat and mix everything evenly.
5. Return the empty saucepan to medium heat (no need to wipe it out). Add ¼ cup water, the ground chicken, and the remaining 1 tablespoon fish sauce. Cook, stirring to break up the chicken, until cooked through, about 4 minutes. Remove from the heat and use the slotted spoon to scoop the chicken into the bowl with the shrimp and noodles and toss once more.
6. Divide the yum woon sen among four bowls and top with chopped peanuts and cilantro before serving.

Chicken Feet Curry

My college roommate was Thai, and when she left Chicago to move back to Florida, I went to visit her. Her mom made chicken feet curry, which was a first for me. But I was in heaven! In the United States, we're used to having our meat processed so it looks nothing like the animal it came from, but there's no avoiding that when it comes to chicken feet. They can be found in many Asian grocery stores. After simmering, they soak up the curry and melt in your mouth with a tender, gelatin-rich texture. Plus, they're packed with collagen, so you're basically eating your way to eternal youth. Who needs a spa day when you've got chicken feet?

Kosher salt

2 pounds chicken feet, nails trimmed, rinsed thoroughly

2 (13.5-ounce) cans full-fat coconut milk

1 cup chicken broth

2 tablespoons vegetable oil or other neutral oil

¼ cup red curry paste

1 (14-ounce) can bamboo shoots, drained

FOR SERVING

Sliced fresh red chiles

Fresh cilantro leaves

Fresh Thai basil leaves

Cooked white rice (see page 175)

1. Bring a large pot of salted water to a boil over high heat. Add the feet and cook until foam rises to the surface, about 5 minutes. Drain and rinse thoroughly with cold water.

2. Wash and dry the pot, then return the feet to it and add the coconut milk, broth, and a good pinch of salt. Bring to a boil over high heat, then cover, reduce the heat to low, and simmer until the feet are tender, 30 to 45 minutes. Set a strainer over a medium bowl. Pour the feet into the strainer, letting the liquid gather in the bowl.

3. Wash and dry the pot again. Heat the vegetable oil over medium heat until it shimmers. Add the curry paste and cook, stirring, until very fragrant, about 2 minutes. Add the reserved coconut liquid one ladleful at a time, stirring continuously to make a smooth sauce. When all the liquid has been incorporated, stir in the chicken feet and bamboo shoots. Simmer, stirring occasionally, until everything is coated and warmed through, about 5 minutes.

4. Divide the curry among four bowls and top with chiles, cilantro, and basil. Serve each portion with a small bowl of rice on the side.

Moo Ping

Moo ping, or Thai grilled pork skewers, are not always easy to find at Thai restaurants outside of Thailand, which is why I knew I needed to learn to make them myself. Once you try them, you're going to want them in your life forever, too. Thai vendors slowly grill the skewers over hot coals until the marinated pork is charred and dripping with juice, and the scent is wafting all across the market. This version is made in the oven, which tastes just as good, but you could always throw these on the grill for a version closer to the original.

2 pounds pork butt or pork shoulder

½ cup unsweetened coconut cream

4 garlic cloves, grated

2 tablespoons palm sugar or light brown sugar

1 tablespoon fish sauce

1 tablespoon soy sauce

1 tablespoon oyster sauce

2 teaspoons white pepper

Chile-Vinegar Sauce (recipe opposite), for serving

Lime wedges, for serving

1. Place the pork in the freezer for about 30 minutes to firm up. Use a very sharp knife to cut the pork into quarters, then slice each quarter against the grain into thin strips.
2. In a large zip-top bag, combine the coconut cream, garlic, palm sugar, fish sauce, soy sauce, oyster sauce, and white pepper. Seal the bag and shake to combine. Add the pork and shake again to coat. Lay the bag flat in the refrigerator and marinate for at least 4 hours and up to 2 days.
3. Preheat the oven to 350°F. Line a rimmed baking sheet with aluminum foil and set a wire rack on top. Soak 12 wooden skewers in plenty of water for at least 30 minutes before using.
4. Remove one piece of pork from the marinade, allowing the excess to drip off. Spear one end of a pork strip with a skewer, then fold and thread it a few more times to make a "ribbon." Continue threading, pushing the pork three-quarters of the way down the skewer to condense, until the skewer is full, then place on the prepared wire rack. Continue with the remaining pork and skewers. Brush the skewers with the leftover marinade.
5. Bake the pork for about 40 minutes, flipping and basting with the marinade every 5 minutes for the first 20 minutes, until the pork is charred and tender. Discard any leftover marinade.
6. Transfer the skewers to a serving platter. Serve immediately with the chile-vinegar sauce for dipping and plenty of lime wedges for squeezing.

Chile-Vinegar Sauce

MAKES 1½ CUPS

- ¼ cup distilled white vinegar
- 2 tablespoons fish sauce
- 1½ teaspoons palm sugar or light brown sugar
- 1 garlic clove, grated
- 1 fresh Thai chile, stemmed and minced

In a small bowl, whisk together the vinegar, fish sauce, palm sugar, garlic, and chile until the sugar has dissolved. Cover with plastic wrap and refrigerate until ready to serve, up to 3 days.

Pink Milk

Pink milk, or nom yen, is Thailand's ultimate summer refresher. The bright sala syrup, made from an extract of sala fruit, has a sweet, fragrant, slightly tart flavor, and it gives the drink a bubblegum hue that's basically my dream blush shade. It's mixed with either fresh milk or sweetened condensed milk and is served ice cold to combat humid Thai afternoons. I love it as a pretty summer drink.

- 1 cup sala syrup, plus more for serving
- 1 (14-ounce) can sweetened condensed milk
- 1 (12-ounce) can evaporated milk
- Ice, for serving

1. Chill 6 tall glasses in the refrigerator for about 1 hour before serving.
2. In a large pitcher, whisk together the sala syrup, condensed milk, evaporated milk, and 2 cups warm water to incorporate well.
3. Drizzle a little sala syrup inside the chilled glasses, then fill with plenty of ice. Pour the pink milk into the glasses, dividing evenly, and serve immediately.

Curry Fish Balls

These fish balls can be found in street markets all over Hong Kong, drenched in curry sauce and served on skewers. Fish balls are basically the equivalent of hot dogs: Don't worry about what's in them; just know it's fish and they're delicious. They're a perfect street snack because they're filling, always served in generous portions, and super cheap. And they're a perfect at-home snack, too, because they're quick to make and easy to keep on hand—whenever I'm in an Asian grocery store, I grab a bag of fish balls so they're in my freezer ready to go!

- 2 tablespoons vegetable oil or other neutral oil
- 1 medium yellow onion, thinly sliced
- 8 garlic cloves, minced
- 1 tablespoon curry powder
- 1 tablespoon ketchup
- 1 tablespoon soy sauce
- 1 teaspoon kosher salt
- 1 teaspoon sugar
- 1 teaspoon chicken bouillon
- 2 tablespoons unsalted butter
- 2 tablespoons heavy cream
- 1 (8-ounce) package fish balls (about 20)

1. In a large skillet, heat the vegetable oil over medium heat until it shimmers. Add the onions and garlic and cook, stirring often, until the onions are soft, about 5 minutes. Stir in the curry powder until fragrant, about 30 seconds.
2. Carefully transfer the mixture to a blender and add the ketchup, soy sauce, salt, sugar, chicken bouillon, and 2 cups water. Blend on high speed until smooth, about 1 minute. Return the curry sauce to the skillet over medium heat. When the sauce is simmering, add the butter and cream and whisk until fully incorporated. Cook until slightly thickened, another 5 minutes.
3. Rinse the fish balls under cold water. Add them to the sauce, cover, and simmer until warmed through, about 10 minutes. Serve the fish balls directly from the skillet with toothpicks or wooden skewers for spear-fish(ball)ing.

Tomato Ramen

Hong Kong has one of the most vibrant food scenes in Asia, with incredible street markets and restaurants at every price point. Because the real estate can be so expensive, and apartments can be very small, a lot of people choose to eat out for their meals. This tomato ramen is an especially popular choice for something filling and cheap. The stalls that sell this will load the bowl up with your choice of ramen, macaroni, Spam, fried eggs, chicken wings, and sliced meat. When I'm making it, it's the perfect excuse to use up scraps of all the things I have lingering in the fridge.

- 1 (14.5-ounce) can diced tomatoes
- 3 tablespoons soy sauce
- 1 (3-ounce) package instant ramen noodles, flavor packet discarded
- 2 slices Spam or firm tofu, drained
- 1 tablespoon vegetable oil or other neutral oil
- 1 large egg

FOR SERVING

- Thinly sliced scallions
- Chile oil
- Toasted sesame seeds

1. In a blender, combine the tomatoes and their juices, the soy sauce, and 1 cup water. Blend on high speed to form a smooth broth, about 1 minute.

2. Pour the tomato broth into a small saucepan. Bring to a simmer over medium heat and cook until reduced by roughly a third, about 10 minutes. Drop the ramen noodles and Spam into the simmering broth. Cook, stirring occasionally, until the noodles are tender and the Spam is warmed through, 3 to 4 minutes.

3. Meanwhile, in a small nonstick skillet, heat the vegetable oil over medium heat until it shimmers. Add the egg and cook without moving it until the white is almost set. Remove from the heat; the hot skillet will continue setting the white.

4. Pour the tomato ramen into a bowl, top with the fried egg, and finish with some scallions, a drizzle of chile oil, and a sprinkle of sesame seeds. Serve immediately.

Milk Tea Ice Pops

Hong Kong's milk tea is legendary. It was a tradition inherited from British colonization, when the afternoon cuppa with sugar and milk was adapted to Hong Kong-style tea using cans of sweetened condensed and evaporated milk instead. Sounds like a perfect dessert to me, so I thought it would be fun to capture the essence of the signature drink in an ice pop form.

1 (12-ounce) can evaporated milk

1½ cups whole milk

18 black tea bags

1 (14-ounce) can sweetened condensed milk

1. In a small saucepan, bring the evaporated milk and whole milk to a gentle simmer over medium heat. Remove from the heat and stir in the tea bags. Cover and let steep for about 30 minutes.
2. Uncover the pan and discard the tea bags. Stir in the condensed milk, then cover again and let sit at room temperature for another 30 minutes.
3. Stir the mixture. In a set of 10 ice pop molds (see Note), pour the mixture almost to the top of each. Set the sticks in the molds and freeze overnight.
4. When ready to serve, run the molds under warm water to help release the ice pops.

NOTE If you don't have ice pop molds, use 8-ounce paper or plastic cups, filled about halfway. Freeze for about 2 hours, until semi-firm, then insert wooden sticks before freezing overnight.

Grilled Milk Toast

Most vendors who sell tomato ramen (see page 195) will also sell a simple slice of milk toast as a side to eat with it. It's a sweet accent to the zesty and tangy tomato broth. In other parts of the city, in the diner-café hybrid known as cha chaan teng, a more presentational version of milk toast is a popular option after a night out or first thing in the morning—two thick slices of bread held together with peanut butter, deep-fried, and drizzled with sweetened condensed milk. When I'm at home, I like to treat it more like a massive piece of French toast with a quick buttery pan-fry for a similar effect.

- 2 slices plain Texas toast
- 1 tablespoon creamy peanut butter
- 1 tablespoon sweetened condensed milk, plus more for serving
- 1 large egg
- ½ cup vegetable oil or other neutral oil
- Unsalted butter, for serving

1. Lay the bread slices on a cutting board. Spread the peanut butter on one slice and the condensed milk on the other. Press the slathered sides of the slices together and cut the crusts off the sandwich.
2. Beat the egg in a shallow bowl. Dip the sandwich into the egg, turning to coat and letting it absorb the egg.
3. In a medium skillet, heat the vegetable oil over medium heat until it shimmers. Add the sandwich and cook until golden brown all over, about 2 minutes per side.
4. Transfer the toast to a plate, drizzle with condensed milk, and finish with a pat of butter before serving.

Dahi Puri

I first saw dahi puri while I was walking around the streets of Mumbai and was immediately curious. It's a puffed cracker stuffed with cooling yogurt, spicy chutneys, and crunchy veggies and topped with sev, those little fried chickpea noodles that make every bite better. When I got back to LA, I was craving that flavor and found the puri shells in an Indian grocery along with all the chutneys, spices, and sev I need to throw together a plate of my favorite street snack anytime!

- 1 medium russet potato, peeled and diced
- ½ cup plain full-fat yogurt (not Greek)
- 1 teaspoon sugar
- ½ teaspoon kosher salt
- 12 puri shells
- 1 small red onion, diced
- 1 vine tomato, diced

FOR SERVING

- Green chutney
- Tamarind chutney
- Ground cumin
- Chaat masala
- Finely chopped fresh cilantro
- Pomegranate seeds
- Sev

1. Place the potatoes in a small saucepan and add enough cold water to cover. Bring to a boil over high heat. Cook until the potatoes are fork-tender, about 3 minutes, then drain and let cool.
2. In a small bowl, whisk together the yogurt, sugar, and salt.
3. To assemble, lightly press your thumb on the top of each puri shell to crack it and make a small hole. Fill the shell with a couple pieces of potato, a few pieces of onion and tomato, and a spoonful of the seasoned yogurt. Arrange the filled shells on a serving plate.
4. Just before serving, spoon a little green and tamarind chutney in each shell. Sprinkle cumin and chaat masala on top, then garnish with cilantro, pomegranate seeds, and sev.

Chana Chaat

Move over, boring bean salads. This chickpea salad is spicy, zesty, and anything but ordinary. The fresh mix of chickpeas, vegetables, sliced chile, and toasted spices makes it more exciting than your typical bean salad. The key ingredient is chaat masala, a floral, slightly tart spice blend popular in Indian cuisine that really pulls it all together. I love to eat this salad as a light lunch or serve it as a perfect side to grilled meats.

- 2 tablespoons vegetable oil or other neutral oil
- 2 (15.5-ounce) cans chickpeas, drained and rinsed
- 1 cup raw cashews
- 1 teaspoon ground cumin
- 1 teaspoon chaat masala
- 1 teaspoon kosher salt
- 1 small red onion, thinly sliced
- 1 mini or Persian cucumber, thinly sliced
- 1 green chile or serrano pepper, stemmed, seeded, and thinly sliced
- 2 tablespoons finely chopped fresh cilantro
- Juice of 1 lemon

1. In a large skillet, heat the vegetable oil over medium heat until it shimmers. Add the chickpeas, cashews, cumin, chaat masala, and salt. Cook, stirring, until the chickpeas are just barely warmed through, about 3 minutes. Transfer to a medium bowl. Let cool to room temperature if desired.

2. Just before serving, add the onions, cucumbers, chiles, cilantro, and lemon juice and toss to combine well.

Yogurt Rice

Most fans of Indian food know all about samosas, chicken biryani, and saag paneer, among other classics found on most menus. But I am fascinated by the simple staple dishes made and served in homes everywhere—the kind you won't find in restaurants because they're not fancy enough. This yogurt rice is a perfect example. In high school, whenever I would go over to one of my friend's homes, her mom would feed me bowls upon bowls of this rice dish. It's tangy, savory, super filling, and perfectly cooling on a hot day or alongside an extra spicy entrée.

- 1 cup basmati rice
- ½ cup unsweetened shredded coconut
- 1 (1-inch) piece fresh ginger, peeled and grated
- 1 cup whole milk
- 1 cup plain full-fat yogurt (not Greek)
- ½ English cucumber, diced
- 1 teaspoon kosher salt
- 1 tablespoon vegetable oil or other neutral oil
- 1 dried red chile, such as Guntur Sannam or chile de árbol, snapped in half
- 8 fresh curry leaves, torn in half
- ¼ cup roasted cashews, coarsely chopped
- 1 green chile or serrano pepper, stemmed, seeded, and thinly sliced
- ¼ cup chopped fresh cilantro

1. In a small bowl, rinse the rice under cold water, swishing it to release the starch, and drain several times until the water runs mostly clear. In a medium saucepan, bring 1½ cups water to a boil over high heat. Stir in the rice, cover, and reduce the heat to low. Simmer until the rice is tender, about 15 minutes. Remove from the heat and stir in the coconut and ginger. Cover and let the rice steam for 10 minutes.

2. Stir the milk, yogurt, cucumbers, and salt into the rice mixture. Transfer to a serving bowl and smooth into an even layer. Let sit for about 5 minutes to thicken.

3. Meanwhile, in a small skillet, heat the vegetable oil over medium heat until it shimmers. Add the dried chile, curry leaves, and cashews and cook, stirring continuously, until the leaves are fragrant, 30 to 60 seconds. Spoon the mixture over the rice. Finish with the green chiles and cilantro and serve immediately.

Dal Tadka

Dal tadka is my go-to order at any Indian restaurant. It's a thick blend of split pigeon peas and spices, rich but not too heavy, spiced but not overwhelming, and it just makes you feel good. The best part is you can't mess it up. Overcooked pigeon peas are exactly what you want! The legume starches thicken the liquid into a creamy consistency. So let it simmer away, and your whole house will smell heavenly.

DAL

- 1 cup toor dal (split pigeon peas)
- 1 tablespoon vegetable oil or other neutral oil
- 1 medium white onion, diced
- 1 (1-inch) piece fresh ginger, peeled and minced
- 2 garlic cloves, minced
- 1 green chile or serrano pepper, stemmed, seeded, and minced
- 1 teaspoon cumin seeds
- ½ teaspoon ground turmeric
- ½ teaspoon garam masala
- 2 vine tomatoes, diced
- 1 teaspoon kosher salt, plus more as needed
- 2 tablespoons chopped fresh cilantro

TADKA

- 3 tablespoons vegetable oil or other neutral oil
- 1 teaspoon cumin seeds
- 2 dried red chiles, such as Guntur Sannam or chiles de árbol, snapped in half
- 3 garlic cloves, minced

1. **Make the dal:** In a small bowl, rinse the toor dal under cold water, rubbing it as you rinse. Drain well, then fill the bowl with hot water. Soak for 30 minutes and drain again.

2. In a large Dutch oven, combine the dal and 4 cups water. Bring to a boil over high heat, then reduce the heat to low and cook until the dal is starting to break apart, about 30 minutes. Periodically use a wooden spoon to skim off and discard any foam from the surface. Remove from the heat and use the spoon to lightly mash the dal against the sides of the pot, keeping some texture.

3. In a small saucepan, heat the vegetable oil over medium heat until it shimmers. Add the onions, ginger, garlic, and chiles. Cook, stirring often, until the onions are soft, about 3 minutes. Stir in the cumin seeds, turmeric, and garam masala and cook until fragrant, about 30 seconds. Add the tomatoes and salt. Simmer, stirring occasionally, until the tomatoes start to break down, about 8 minutes.

4. Stir the tomato mixture into the dal. Return the Dutch oven to medium heat and simmer until the flavors have melded, about 8 minutes. Taste and adjust the seasoning. Stir in the cilantro and remove from the heat again.

5. **Make the tadka:** Wipe out the small saucepan, add the vegetable oil, and return to medium heat until it shimmers. Add the cumin seeds and dried chiles. Cook, stirring continuously, until fragrant, about 1 minute. Stir in the garlic and immediately remove from the heat.

6. Divide the dal among four bowls and spoon the tadka over the top. Serve immediately.

Mango Pudding

They treated us so well on tour in India—in every city, the hotel rooms would be fully stocked with snacks, and mango pudding was always one of them. I don't like complicated desserts, so when I came across that sweet pudding, I knew I wanted to bring it back home with me. Besides, I got hooked on eating my daily fix! Frozen mango is my secret move, since I know it will be as ripe and flavorful as Indian mango every time.

1 (13.5-ounce) can full-fat coconut milk

Juice of 2 limes

½ cup sugar

3 cups frozen chopped mango, thawed, plus more for serving

1 teaspoon ground cardamom

1 tablespoon plus 1 teaspoon agar-agar powder, or 2 tablespoons cornstarch

Unsweetened shredded coconut, for serving

1. In a blender, combine the coconut milk, lime juice, sugar, mango, and cardamom. Blend on high speed until smooth, about 2 minutes.
2. In a small saucepan, whisk the agar-agar with ½ cup water. Cook over low heat, whisking often, until the mixture is thick like jelly, 6 to 8 minutes. Pour the mixture into the blender with the coconut mixture and blend on medium until smooth.
3. Pour the pudding into four 8-ounce ramekins or drinking glasses. Press plastic wrap directly on the surface of the pudding and chill in the refrigerator to set for at least 2 hours and up to 3 days.
4. Just before serving, discard the plastic and arrange a few pieces of mango and a sprinkle of coconut on the surface of each pudding.

Recipes by Category

Recipes by Ingredient

Acknowledgments

First of all, thank you to everyone who believes in me and loves me enough to come see me! Without your support, I wouldn't get to do what I do and experience the amazing culture all around the world.

Thank you to everyone over at team VOSS for having my back all these years, always being my biggest supporters, and organizing my hectic life.

Everyone on team KimChi Chic Beauty, I am so lucky to be able to work with such talented, kind, and hardworking folks. You mean the world to me!

Casey Elsass, where do I even begin? The best collaborator anyone could ask for! It's always a pleasure to chat with you and have a chance to experience your knowledge and wisdom. Working relationship aside, you are a phenomenal person, and I hope you'll be in my life after this project!

Andrea D'Agosto, you are a true visionary, and I love that you celebrate all things fun, weird, and quirky, aka my vision for this book! You deserve all the success! I've had a blast working on this book with you. The long shoot days never felt long because I was having so much fun. Honestly, anyone in the food space who hasn't gotten a chance to work with you is seriously missing out.

Tyna Hoang, I think I gained so many pounds during the shoot because every dish you styled was presented beautifully and immaculately and also seasoned so perfectly. Eating my own food in the hands of a true professional, I am living the life.

Ruth Kim. A true artist. The way you were able to understand my offbeat and colorful vision and executed the styling in such a masterful way—I still get chills thinking about your effortless ability to marry different colors, textures, and patterns. Watching you styling was truly a life-changing experience.

To my dear Juanita More!, thank you for always keeping me on your guest list.

Amanda Englander and Juliana Nador, you folks are the best editors a queen can ask for! Thank you for taking a chance on this lil dainty queen and making my cookbook dream come true.

David Purse, for reaching out to me and making all this magic happen! We are all here today thanks to you!

Now for my personal loved ones. Y'all already know I'm bad at being sentimental and sappy. I suppose I could use this time to be *~vulnerable~* and tell you how I really feel. I'm already cringing and you probably are, too. Well, here goes nothing:

To my family, my life experience as a Korean American would not be possible without everything we've gone through together, and for that I am forever grateful.

Naomi Smalls, the best judy anyone could ever ask for. I hope our chat history never gets leaked.

My other drag queen friends and sisters who might've gotten canceled at one point or another (you know who you are), thanks for the glam, laughter, and many, many shady screen shots.

Diana and Mo, Butter and I are so lucky to have y'all in our lives!

LA ajummas (you know who you are), I enjoy growing old with you and eating too much meat.

Godoy, thanks for always making me look fabulous no matter what and taking on whatever stupid concepts I come up with, plus always being 100% chaotic.

Group chat gaysians (you know who you are), shabu date soon with your foreheads? Board game gaymers (you know who you are), never in my life did I expect to meet so many people with the same interests as mine while being fabulously gay. I learn so much from y'all while having so much fun! LA foodie friends (you know who you are), what's the next spot? When are we going? SF gaysians (you know who you are), see you in August.

Jon, thank you for everything.

Khushbu, thanks for being so pure . . . Michigan.

Butter, for being the best dog in the world and always loving me unconditionally . . . until a friend visits our home.

Index

NOTE: Page numbers in *italics* refer to photos of recipes.

C

D

E

F

G

H

I

J

K

L

M

N

O

P

Q

R

S

T

U

V

W

Y